Make Money
The slow and effective way

*Everything you don't want to hear
from your older brother*

Bill Silverstone

Copyright © 2020 by Bill Silverstone

All rights reserved.

No part of this book may be reproduced in any form or by any electronic or mechanical means, including information storage and retrieval systems, without written permission from the author, except for the use of brief quotations in a book review.

ISBN: 979-8-55-943496-4

Editor: Hannah McAuliffe, https://www.hannahmcauliffe.com

INDEX

Preface 6
The structure of this book 8

LEVEL 1
1. **The world's gone bananas** 13
   - Buffer overflow
   - Shelves within a bookshelf within a library
   - Between Stimulus and Response
   - OK, but the world's really gone bananas
   - The starting point

2. **Your job** 26
   - Find a job
   - Keep your job or change it but do not lose it

3. **Willpower, Choices, and the Brain** 36
   - Willpower
   - Choices
   - The Brain

4. **The case for saving and investing** 40
   - The richest dad in Babylon
   - Xiaohui and Jenny
   - Save some more money - NOW!

5. **The First House** 50
   - Why you should invest in a property
   - The importance of criteria
   - Some final points

6. **Preparing to go Beyond** 57
   - Recap
   - Between Level 1 and Level 2
   - Level 2
   - Put your standard finances in order
   - Sustainability, minimalism and frugality
   - Specialisation

LEVEL 2
7. **Your Own Business** 73
   - The world is full of money
   - From Tax Free to Sole Trader
   - Paperwork, Admin and Practicalities

Congratulations! You now have a business!

8. 發, Growing Wealth   84
    A real story of money and life
    The reality of paperwork
    Your first Buy-to-Let: Decision and Analysis
    Your first Buy-to-Let: Purchase and Renting

INTERPHASE (THE THEORY)   105
    MOTIVATION
    EATING FROGS
    THE VERT
    MAKING AND BREAKING THE GRID
    LIFE AND BUSINESS QUOTES

INTERPHASE (THE PRACTICE)   119
    MORTGAGES
    KEEPING ORDER: PRACTICAL TIPS
    THE CREATOR
    WEBSITE AND MARKETING
    PERSONAL DEVELOPMENT

Level 1 and Level 2 – To do list   136

LEVEL 3
9. The Junction
    Your properties   141
    Your business
    Yourself
    Your Connections
    Final thoughts on The Junction

10. Your real business   162
    Your job and your business
    Your product/service
    How do you get your customers?
    Data and Systems
    Managing complexity
    Mind your business
    Summary

11. The art of selling   196
    The importance of sales
    Practical selling

12. The switch						218

LEVEL 4
13. The devil is in the detail				225
    Income Tax – Basics
    Incomes, properties and taxes
    The Company
    International dreams and taxes

LEVEL 5
Conclusion						239

Preface

From around 2006 and after realising that a Bachelor's degree in International Relations in Italy wasn't going to magically turn me into an ambassador or even a diplomat, mainly given my lack of connections and willingness to become part of a certain world and *modus operandi,* I started to walk the long and difficult road to financial independence. This road is not difficult *per se* but, unless you have some guidance and idea of the concepts, navigating the world of money, investment, business and taxation can be daunting and confusing.

This book is mainly aimed at people in their twenties and early thirties and it seeks to give you some useful ideas and practical guidance on how to make money.

I also used to be twenty years old, with vague dreams and aspirations, with the blissful ignorance of the systems that are already in place, which invites you to see opportunities where, in fact, there are none. I myself have grandiosely ignored common knowledge, made bad choices and walked at night through Rome, Beijing and London looking for something which I could not clearly define while partying with friends and strangers.

Happening to be in my twenties between 2004 and 2014, I've had the honour of observing the apex of the 'globalification' (globalisation and californication) and its demise in the financial crash of 2008, followed by the boring years that followed in Europe and the US. Being an economic migrant, but also a member of the middle class, I understand why it can be difficult to establish yourself in another country and why it can be frustrating to see how much we have to struggle compared with the previous generation. All in a world that's changing, and will continue to change, at an ever-increasing speed.

In this book I want to share with you what I've learnt so far, help you to really understand the nitty-gritty of business, investment and money, and propose a strategy that has worked – and is still working – for me, my wife and many other people.

While this journey is far from over, after fourteen years, many mistakes, some good luck, and some interesting experiences, I think I'm finally grasping the real nature of money, business, busyness, and investment.
Over the course of the last decade I've read many books about sales, business, self-improvement and so forth. While many are very interesting and offer some excellent points, they all have the same problem: they're written either by people who have experienced a very specific set of circumstances, or by people who are so high up they struggle to communicate with us mere mortals. In some cases, these books are written by people who don't even have first-hand experience of many of the things they're talking about!

The idea for this book came in the spring of 2020, during the Coronavirus pandemic, while talking with my younger brother who has a very different outlook on life. While he understands the brutal logic behind some of my statements, he philosophically disagrees with some of my basic assumptions on life and human nature, and cannot accept some of the compromises that are required to make money.

So, I was sitting on a sofa talking about money and investment when he said: "you should write a book titled, 'Everything you don't want to hear from your older brother'". My answer was: "that sounds like a good idea," and because I've always emphasised to him the importance of implementation, I sat down and wrote it all within two months.

I hope you will enjoy these pages and good luck with your journey towards wealth.

Why should I trust you?

In this book I'll be as practical as possible, however, some explanations and theoretical frameworks are necessary to understand the world and what I will say. Moreover, before even beginning to suggest what you should do, what kind of mystical mindset you should develop, how to perfect yourself, how to win friends through Neuro-Linguistic Programming, or how to work four hours a week, let's do something more important: let's establish some sort of credibility… and by the way, you will never work only four hours a week, just forget about it, OK?

It is now 2020-2021. The world is struggling with the Coronavirus outbreak and I'm comfortably writing from my house in the North of England, the nation where the Industrial Revolution started. I'm also aware that I could lose my job and still survive comfortably for years and years.

At the moment, I have three houses (one to live in and two to let), a car which was paid off almost three years ago, a business that's bringing in money, a full-time job, and a wife who has lost her job as the result of Coronavirus and found another a few days later. We've been able to build our net-worth from £20,000 to upwards of £300,000 within seven years, and we're not too worried about the future, even if there is the Coronavirus-induced recession on the horizon and Brexit is a fact. On the contrary, we're rather busy making more and more money at an ever-increasing speed.

I'm originally from the south of Italy, my family has supported me throughout my studies and for a short while after. I have a Master's degree in International Relations which is the most useful-useless skill I have, I've tried to speak various languages for many years, my passions include inline skating and aggressive skating (but I've never been brave enough to start to grind), web design, politics, and science at large. When I came to England in February 2010, I had 2,000 euros that my parents gave me after graduation, a heavy grey suitcase which is now in the garage at the back of my home, and an Acer Aspire laptop which I still use nowadays to watch anime online while we have dinner.

I'm not a poor migrant from sub-Saharan Africa who has become a millionaire nor the son of millionaires, I'm not a genius nor an idiot, but I'm somewhere in the middle of all these things: a middle class guy from a standard family from southern Europe who has been living abroad for ten years and is on his way to complete financial independence and freedom. Most of us start somewhere there, in the middle, which can sometimes make things all the more complicated.

The previous paragraphs are not intended to boast about what I consider the underachievements of an overqualified person (many mistakes were made along the way!), nor to be disrespectful to people who are struggling because of the Coronavirus, or Brexit, or any other mess that history throws at us. Rather, it's to give you some context and a sense of what this book is about: realistic expectations and realistic growth that can be achieved in a reasonable amount of time with dedication, compromise, but also luck and support.

This book is NOT about how to make five million dollars in two years, nor about how you can become a real estate millionaire investor in thirty years and then die. My aim here is to describe the lessons that I've learnt about money, business and human nature; and share them with my younger brother, and with you, too; and, in the process, hopefully sell some books and make some more money…obviously!

The structure of this book

In order for you to get a feeling about the natural development of money and the skills that you need to make, grow and, most importantly, keep it, I have divided this book into 'Levels' rather than topics. This means you will *not* be administered a dose of ideas on certain topics in an encyclopedic fashion (money, property investment, business), but you'll follow a storyline of sorts, where you can see why certain choices are made at certain points and their implications, from Level 1 to Level 5 . Towards the end of the book I will also emphasise some of the mistakes that most of us without guidance make, so you'll know what to avoid when structuring your wealth.
The whole book revolves around the idea that, in order to make money, you'll need to have a mix of four things: a job where you learn something new every day, properties, your own business and investments and, last but by no means least, your own network and motivation for self-development. This means that, for most levels, we will cover one or more of these topics and jump from business to properties, from investment to self-development.

Certainly there are many examples of people who have become millionaires or even billionaires by simply investing in properties, others that have devoted all their energies to their business idea, or the implementation of that idea, and others that have become very highly paid consultants using their skills and knowledge. If you are so inclined, and prefer to focus on just one thing, feel free to do so but please bear in mind that if it fails, you may have lost precious time. On the other hand, if it works, you'll probably make more money than by sinking your time and energy into many different things. It's a matter of personal choice and propensity to risk.

If you follow the ideas shared in this book, I am sure that, sooner or later, you will reach that turning point where you are *truly* financially independent.

By the way, when I say "financially independent" I mean that you could lose your job but still live until the end of your life with no problems at all because you have your own business, rental incomes, investments and, above all, the skills to make more money than you spend every day, month and year.

Below is a very schematic overview of the different Levels:

- Level 1 – Keep/find/improve your job and buy your first home
- Level 2 – Invest in more properties and start your own business
- Level 3 – Grow your wealth
- Level 4 – Taxes, international business, and properties
- Level 5 – Going beyond

IMPORTANT NOTICE!

This book is PACKED with concepts, ideas and information. If you just read it, you'll get the feeling of understanding it, but you'll forget 80% of what you read. In order to fully absorb this information, you should read each page slowly and, where there's a concept or exercise, open your laptop and do the research. There's no magic formula to making money, but there are skills and mindsets you can develop. Also, while we will follow a sort of storyline, as we proceed with the book you'll see that the timing of certain things is important and can be very personal, so the natural development of the storyline is not necessarily the only way to organise (or even grow) your wealth. But you'll know this for sure by the end of this journey and now, let the journey begin.

Level 1

Basics

A journey of a thousand miles begins with a single step
千里之行，始於足下

Chapter 1 – The world's gone bananas

Buffer overflow

The world has gone bananas and we can't escape the context we're living in when we talk about money, business and financial independence.

For at least the last ten to fifteen years, a standard day for many people in the West has gone something like this:

- Wake up, possibly after a night spent sleeping next to a Wi-Fi router
- Check the phone for new messages for a quick dopamine boost
- Head to the kitchen to get some breakfast while reading messages, news or social media
- Shower and get ready for work/study
- Commuting: more news, social media and Candy Crush
- Working/studying at least eight hours per day plus some more news and social media
- Commuting plus some more news and social media
- If the weather's good and you're not too tired or broke, do something outside, perhaps once during the week and once or twice over the weekend - always making sure that there's no breaking news you really need to check or any very important messages you have received
- Sleep
- Repeat

Exercise – Find the problem

While I'm not a big fan of the so-called rat race[1], I think it is still better than the Arms Race[2] that led to World War I. In fact, this rat race channels destructive forces into productive labour. If you're too tired from working and producing goods or services to embrace any strong ideology, while your soul might be annihilated, at least you don't have a bayonet in your stomach. Not great but it's an improvement.

So, what's the real problem in the scheme above?
    a) Too much time spent reading news
    b) Too much time spent on social media
    c) Instant gratification from superfluous communication

---

[1] A way of life in which people are caught up in a fiercely competitive struggle for wealth or power.

[2] A competition between nations for superiority in the development and accumulation of weapons.

- d) Wi-Fi affecting your sleep
- e) Toxicity
- f) The routine
- g) Something else

Obviously, it's the combination of them all, however, there's an extremely important point we need to understand if we want to move forward: the buffer overflow.

From Wikipedia:

"In information security and programming, a buffer overflow, or buffer overrun, is an anomaly where a program, while writing data to a buffer, overruns the buffer's boundary and overwrites adjacent memory locations."

Now, your brain and my brain haven't got any adjacent memory locations to write on, so if you write too much data on them, they will run out of space and processing power to do anything useful.

Let's use an example that could be taken from me a few years ago when my mind was going into buffer overflow. This was pretty much a typical day, probably for many Europeans living in the UK through the days of Brexit, ISIS and Trump.

During the same day I could spend a lot of time and energy thinking about the following things:

- I'm getting bold, I'm getting old, my belly is growing, what the hell is that speck in my eye?! Go back to your own country!
- What will happen to the pound if A, B and C happens?
- Should I move the euro into pounds or vice versa?
- The radicalisation of young Muslims that are getting brainwashed by ISIS
- The growth of extreme-right among disenfranchised white teenagers
- I need to renegotiate my mortgage
- What happens if I lose my job? What about my wife's job?
- We want to go on holidays in a hot place
- That porn star is hot! Damn! She died of an overdose
- Melting permafrost, CO_2 being released into the atmosphere
- Coral reef bleaching
- Why did they vote for the guy who speaks strangely?
- Is it safer to drink bottled water or tap water? How much microplastic have I ingested today?
- Should I switch banks? Interest rates are so low... should I save or overpay the mortgage?

- Perhaps I should have studied engineering?

...and so on.

Basically, my mind was getting overwhelmed by the sheer amount of stimulus, information, news and doubts that the Internet and media was throwing at us. Processing all this information was taking a lot of time and energy and, while I was still able to process most of it and obtain some results, it was all done in a very inefficient way.

In his masterpiece, 'The 7 Habits of Highly Effective People,' Mr. Covey provides a particularly useful mental tool: the Circle of Influence and the Circle of Concern.

Broadly speaking there are two kind of things:

- things we are concerned about but over which we have no influence and
- things we can influence

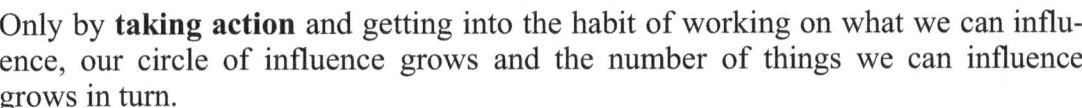

and we should focus most of our attention on the **things we can influence**.

Only by **taking action** and getting into the habit of working on what we can influence, our circle of influence grows and the number of things we can influence grows in turn.

This is one of the most important teachings of Mr. Covey.

We can **worry** about the melting permafrost in Russian Siberia, but if we worry, we're not actually doing anything. On the other hand, if we decide to walk to work or to the supermarket, we're implementing a specific action to obtain a result.

We can worry about our health or we can go out for a run (with the right shoes); we can worry about our jobs or we can work much harder or change jobs; we can worry about our skills or we can go and learn new skills.

When you are worried.... ACT!

Having said that, this book is not about 'how to change the world', so you should learn to be selective with what you decide to worry about and act on, and learn the art of completely ignoring most of what's not strictly relevant to you. First become independent, *then* save the world.

Exercise – Mind cleansing

In this exercise we will go through what's going on in our minds and then you should decide:

- what to act on
- what to discard
- what to postpone

Now, this is the kind of exercise that people will skip since many of you are looking for a holy grail of knowledge on how to make money quickly and without efforts, which clearly does not exist.

This is not a one-off exercise; it should be a tool for you to use every now and then. Let's do this exercise together and please, do it, **do not just read it**!

Let's write down the main thoughts we have in our minds today and decide which ones to focus on by making them bold or underlined. You should write on the book since you will not sell it on and it will be useful for years to come.

My thoughts

- Should I publish this anonymously?
- Am I wasting time and not focusing on my business?
- I must submit paperwork for my business
- Should I pay some more money to that freelancer?
- Is the work on the company website proceeding?
- I want to go on holiday but there's coronavirus
- If it rains, I can't go on the half-pipe with my inline skates
- I need another order before the end of the summer
- **I need to visit the doctor**
- I would like to overpay my mortgage even more
- There's a coronavirus second wave in Leicester
- Will my brother be overcharged on rent in a few months?
- **I need to finish the material to send to the freelancer for the new website**
- It would be good to put a   between the mathematical symbols and the numbers in the HTML code
- I want a landline number for my website in Italy
- It would be good to write an article on a specific topic and link it via Wikipedia for SEO (Search Engine Optimisation)
- Will my wife lose her job?

Your thoughts

WRITE YOUR THOUGHTS HERE
GO ON... WRITE!

Now, your list will surely be completely different from mine, but I'm quite confident that, as in mine, there will be only a **few elements in bold** (unless you're trying to cheat yourself and pretending to be an over-pragmatic person).

Let's analyse my list first.

Should I publish this anonymously?

Write the book before you worry about this.

Am I wasting time and not focusing on my business?

We all have self-doubt and nothing is certain in life. It's difficult to decide and, very often, the best course of action is to DO, rather than think if you should do it or not.

I must submit paperwork for my business

OK, I am waiting for an activation code from the taxman to do this. Move on.

Should I pay some more money to that freelancer?

Probably, if it's the right thing to do. You want to make money, not at the expense of someone else but by creating an ever-increasing value yourself.

Is the work on the company website proceeding?

Should I really worry about this? During the last week those who are working on it have been far more productive than I have, and I still have many things to do myself!

I want to go on holiday but there's coronavirus.

Tough! Move on.

If it rains, I can't go on the half-pipe with my inline skates

It's raining now – give up.

I need another order before the end of the summer

Yes, and I also need ten million pounds – no need to focus on this, keep focusing on the activities you can do to generate that order.

I need to visit the doctor

OK, put in the agenda that tomorrow I will fix an appointment with my GP.

I would like to overpay my mortgage even more

Already overpaid £12,000; cannot overpay more without incurring a penalty; there's coronavirus so we need more cash in the bank; stop wasting time fantasising about what could or should be done.

There's a coronavirus second wave in Leicester

I'm in Manchester.

Will my brother be overcharged on rent in a few months?

Not my business.

I need to finish the material to send to the freelancer for the new website

This is important, I need three hours, it's 16:46 now on a Sunday. I'll write this book for another hour and then continue with the material.

It would be good to put a   between the mathematical symbols and the numbers in the HTML code

Good boy, you are clever, now move on - you've already decided that your partner was going to do that – do not repeat the same thing over and over.

I want a landline number for my website in Italy

Same as above.

It would be good to write an article on a specific topic and link it via Wikipedia for SEO (Search Engine Optimisation)

Same as above.

Will my wife lose her job?

This is an interesting one and can give you an insight to our thought process and on how sometimes we worry more than we should. Since I wrote this one month ago (now I'm working on the revision of the first draft of the book) my wife lost her job, found a new job with unsociable hours and moved to yet another job a few days ago with standard working hours Monday to Friday. A perfect example of worrying about something that can be fixed and turning a problem (job loss) into an opportunity (new job with better hours).

So, as we can see from my list and from your list, our head is full of random stuff and even more so now we're in the age of social media, instant messaging and hyperconnectivity. This is also one of the reasons why people are increasingly joining meditation classes to cleanse their minds.

I'm a bit more of a mechanical animal, so the list is good enough for me, but **you must find what works best for you**. Cleanse your mind!

Exercise - Eisenhower's principle

Again, this is an interesting tool to classify thoughts and activities called Eisenhower's principle or matrix. Most of our tasks can be put into one of these four boxes and you want to spend most of your time in box 1 and 2 and as little as possible in 3 and 4.

Important / Urgent	**Important / Not Urgent**
(1) DO NOW	(2) PLAN TO DO
Send prices to your customer; pay bills due tomorrow; check bank details; deliver that product; study for the exam due next week.	Study something useful; do physical exercise; make that long-term investment; carry out those marketing activities for your business; plan the most tax efficient structure.
Not Important / Urgent	**Not Important / Not Urgent**
(3) DELEGATE	(4) ELIMINATE
Vacuum the whole office; rename the documents for no good reason; answer that message from a person you barely know asking for money.	Spam email; random people calling and asking questions for market research; read the Daily Mail; chase people not interested in you; useless meetings.

If there's no structure or plan, most of us will spend time in Box 1, 3 and even 4, and avoid and postpone Box 2, which is usually **the place where most changes in life happen**.

Make a note for this box and think NOW where you would put the tasks that have taken up all your time in the last week.

Exercise – Your Eisenhower's Matrix

Important / Urgent (1) DO NOW	**Important / Not Urgent** (2) PLAN TO DO
Not Important / Urgent (3) DELEGATE	**Not Important / Not Urgent** (4) ELIMINATE

Main message

Block out the noise, focus on concrete actions. Implementation, implementation and more implementation. Focus on what you *can* influence, actively ignore what you cannot. Don't waste time reading **too much** news, social media, and superfluous stuff. Focus on what counts and try to spend as much time as possible doing the Important/Urgent and the Important/Non-Urgent, this is where things happen.

Shelves within a bookshelf within a library

You might have noticed that I did not say: "block out ALL social media, ALL the news, ALL the noise" but I deliberately said, don't spend **too much** time reading **too much** news and social media.

So I'm NOT advocating to completely block out the noise and dive into twenty hours per day working on a single activity so that within a few years you will have reached a magic 10,000 hours of work/study on a subject[3], and have become an expert who can rely on these skills for a living.

Everything that is infeasible is indeed unfeasible.

It doesn't matter how hard I tried, how motivated I was, how determined I have been at a point in time… to focus all my time and energy on one specific subject or skill for days, weeks, months or years is extremely difficult indeed. Us non-geniuses need to stay in the realm of the feasible and reasonable.

Also, the superfluous, is not always superfluous.

Our mind is, in fact, like **a great library** where books are added and lost every day, so you need to keep adding some, even those that might seem useless.

Some people have a big library containing books which are mainly on the same subject and very well organised. For example, someone who has a deep knowledge of Chinese history and Chinese culture might know all the names of the Han emperors, all the phases of the Qin dynasty and, when this person reads something new about Chinese history, he knows on which specific shelf and bookshelf that piece of information goes.

Some other people also have an extensive library, however the knowledge and skills are more varied, so there will be a section for history, one for science, one for AI modelling and then, a very specific one about the lubricants used in industrial machinery. If they were to receive new information about a war happening in the Arabian Peninsula, they might know on which bookshelf to put that information (perhaps the history one) but they haven't got a specific shelf for conflicts in the Arabian Peninsula.

Obviously there are some people who have a small library full of fashion magazines, some who have very few books which are strewn across the floor, and some who go to the library mainly to socialise and get in bed with the owner of the library.

Finally, there are also the library builders, the architects, those who give the planning permissions and those who decide what to publish and what not to publish.
It is my strong belief that we should never stop learning and that the best libraries are those where there are bookshelves for every broad aspect of knowledge, but also have a specialisation in something, as well as including the latest magazines, news and publications. In these libraries there should be a cafeteria where people can talk and discuss and, if the librarians are nice, we might want to get to know them bet-

---

[3] There is a theory according to which, if you spend 10,000 hours on any specific activity you can master it.

ter. Later we might throw a party with the city planners to discuss an expansion project and with the censors to get an idea of what important information is being withheld – not that we would ever reveal secret information!

Main message

Keep your mind open, read more books and, when possible, add **structured knowledge that comes from manuals**: you need a solid bookshelf to put the information on. If I know nothing about renewable energies, I might get an unbelievably valuable piece of information about a new project or technology, but I wouldn't have any idea what to do with it!

Between Stimulus and Response

> "Between stimulus and response there is a space.
> In that space is our power to choose our response.
> In our response lies our growth and our freedom."
>
> Viktor E. Frankl (Holocaust survivor)

Many people still live in a state of stimulus-response, where they react to things without thinking. This state is similar to that of a plant, a bacterium, a virus or most animals, where there is no time for reflection, for thinking, for analysis but just an instinctive knee-jerk reaction.

Sometimes it seems that our hyper-connected yet disconnected world is becoming something of a mix between the *1984* of George Orwell and the *Brave New World* of Huxley; a world where, on one hand the predominant feelings are fear, anger, hate and victory over real (but imaginary) enemies, and, on the other hand, most of these passions and feelings are snuffed out by the drug called soma that makes everybody happy and some sort of orgy-porgy rituals to feel the oneness of humankind[4].

I don't want to digress too much on whether this is the case or not, whether it is a good outcome or not, or even if this interpretation is simply a view that I have today that will change tomorrow – this is not the point. The point for this paragraph, again, is the following:

> "Between stimulus and response there is a space.
> In that space is our power to choose our response.
> In our response lies our growth and our freedom."

---

[4] These are references to two of the main dystopian novels of the last century. In *1984*, a Big Brother controls the masses through the 'telescreen' and propaganda; in *Brave New World*, all human emotions are controlled and balanced through drugs, rituals and conditioning.

And it's how we decide to respond to a view of the world, to our own view of the world, that decides whether we make money or not. This is extremely important in the world gone bananas, we need to choose our responses and to critically think about why certain things are the way they are.

One of the great lessons you learn from studying a degree in International Relations is that, when you see a piece of news, you don't ask yourself: "Oh, what's happening with the world?" but rather: "Why is this piece of news being published? Who is behind it? What is the agenda of this newspaper compared with that other newspaper?"

Most of the time, a piece of news is published to further the interests of a specific group, ideology, party and so on. The choice of the news, wording and images are all aligned to generate a certain feeling which, hopefully (for the publisher), will translate either into:

- A voting decision
- A buying/spending decision
- An action

Main message

Choose your response to people's actions, people's words, people's ideas, news, social media, movies, books, newspapers, radio programmes, YouTube videos etc. Don't simply be a chemical reaction but take the time to reflect on the stimulus and select the reaction which is in your best interest – obviously, **all with the objective of making money**; we're not trying to be deep and philosophical here, but very practical.

Some examples below.

- Someone shares something political you do not agree with on LinkedIn... ignore it. Do not comment, do not share, do not like it. LinkedIn is for professionals and for business, it is not for politics. With politics, religions, sexuality and other subjective topics you can only lose customers, colleagues, friends and you rarely gain anything.
- Your colleague is constantly subjecting you to micro-aggression because you're black, Asian or part of a minority. You can either fight back, win the fight and gain an enemy; you can try to befriend this person; you can simply ignore the micro-aggression, excel at what you do and crush the idiot's ego; you can work on your own business and wealth and become really free.
- You're driving and someone is going deliberately slowly in front of you. You can risk your life overtaking the slow driver; you can change your route; you can risk damage to your car and lose money; you can stop some-

where, eat something nice, make some business calls and resume driving in sixty minutes.
- You saw someone on social media living an amazing life on a boat, in the Caribbean, fishing and scuba diving. You can spend a lot of money to book a holiday there as soon as possible; you can feel sad and depressed; you can decide to invest to create a passive income so that in future you can do that.

And the list goes on, forever and ever.

OK, but the world's really gone bananas

Look, I really do agree with this, 100%. Like you, I'm living through this crazy period of history with AI threatening to take over millions of jobs, multinational companies out of control, climate change out of control, population growth out of control, quantum computers, terrorism, far-right nationalisms, white supremacists, demographic nationalists, coronavirus, dictators looking like superstars, people worrying about selfies while other people die in the Mediterranean, Brexit, India-China tensions, Syrian war, war in Yemen, war on terror, war on people, police brutality, FGM, voodoo dolls, neo-Nazis and many other strange things in what I like to call:
"The circus of humanity"

It is a "circus" because of the abomination that many of those things represent to the rational mind. But at the same time, while a world without all these feelings, ambitions, greed, will of power and irrational acts would be much better, it might end up being very boring and, since we have no choice (we join the circus when we are born), we may as well enjoy the spectacle.

Main message

This is, again, not a book about politics or religion, but it's about money, investment, and business. So, for the scope of this book, my suggestion is: enjoy the spectacle and take part in the circus when you know you can make a **positive difference through your actions**.

The starting point

Sorry, this section is not yet the holy grail of knowledge to get rich quick (which does not even exist), but we're still in the introduction. It's extremely important to be honest with you, the reader, about the starting point of this journey.
Your starting point is different from my starting point, which is different from Putin, Bill Gates, Ford, Mukesh Ambani, Jack Ma, my best friend and so forth. Everybody has a different history, different genetics, different strengths, different motivations.

It's also important to recognise that if you want to start a limited company in the

UK, it takes £18 and 24 hours, if you want to start the same company in Italy it takes 10,000 euros and 30 days.

If you speak with a posh English accent you will have more success doing YouTube videos than if you did the same videos with a strong Spanish accent.

We also shouldn't forget that if you speak three languages, you're in a much better position than if you only speak one language; and that if you're a man in a technical field you have probably an advantage compared with a woman in the same field.

If you, like me, have had supporting parents, you have probably already overcome quite easily a number of obstacles; on the other hand, if like a good friend of mine, your parents were absent, then you will have encountered a harder struggle.

If you're in the middle of Romania it will be more difficult to start and grow an innovative start-up in nano-technologies than if you were in the middle of Tokyo; on the other hand, if you are in the middle of Kazakhstan you might get some opportunities on the new Silk Road.

What I'm trying to say is that, many books on how to make money, written by entrepreneurs and business people in the US and Europe, struggle to recognise the variety of situations around the world and start from the assumption that the system where the reader operates is the capitalistic system, with certainty of the law, low taxation, good infrastructure, English language fluency and so forth.

As a southern Italian who had to work his way up in the UK I can assure you I know how things like accent, heritage, taxation system, law, politics, geo-politics etc. can influence your chances of getting on in life and can make the struggle even harder.

For these reasons I won't paint a rosy picture of sunny uplands and instant riches. On the contrary, I'll get into the nitty-gritty of how to overcome certain obstacles but also how to recognise which obstacles we should overcome and which we should simply avoid.

Main message

Each situation is different, you might have to struggle a lot, your country might make it difficult to do certain things and you'll have to deal with that and find other opportunities. Things won't play out as described in some of the following chapters, but other things will be easier. This is a guideline not a strict plan, it's a way of looking at the numbers rather than the specific numbers to look at.

Basically…good luck!

Chapter 2 - Your job

We have now established that we need to keep our minds open, go on reading and be connected with the world to spot opportunities. At the same time, we don't want to consume or create noise for the sake of it; we realise that each situation is different and that we need **to think before reacting to create some sort of freedom** which will over time increase our circle of influence and make it converge more and more with the circle of concern. We also agree the world's gone bananas and we may as well enjoy the spectacle of the circus while taking business calls.

After all this philosophical stuff there is the reality:

YOUR JOB

You may now be working from home worried about a potential redundancy, or perhaps you have been recently made redundant, or perhaps you're an independent businessperson with a small shop, or an agent, or a programmer, or even a lawyer. It doesn't matter who or where you are. The very first step to make money is a job and, whoever says otherwise is lying and selling dreams. I've already sold you my book, so no need to sell dreams here.

You do need a job and so do I.

If you check on the cover of this book, there is clearly written:

Everything you don't want to hear
from your older brother

This is a nod to my brother who likes fishing and, like a fish trapped in a net, tries to escape reality and looks for alternative ways of living. He's clever so he might end up finding a creative and clever way to live the dream but, so far, I haven't found this magic wand or solution and neither has he.

Most of us do need a job, in fact, I would say that probably 90% of the global adult population needs a job. There's no escaping this reality. We might not like it and we might disagree with the system. We might want to find creative ways to be free from our job very quickly, but the reality is that, **as a starting point**, we generally DO need to have a job and some sort of independence. Unless you're planning to sponge money from your parents, friends or the government for the rest of your life.

I say generally because there will be some people who inherit a real estate portfolio which pays them thousands of dollars per month, so they won't need a job; some geniuses will become rich before they even leave high school or university working on magic projects so they won't need a job; some people will have won the lottery or saved enough money and be so adventurous to simply 'go for it', leave their full-time employment and open their own business straight away – and most will fail.

Unfortunately, dwelling in the realm of mediocracy, or in gentler terms, being part of the middle class, many of us have got too much to lose or don't have enough spare money to heroically 'go for it'. Instead, we're stuck in the middle, with ever-growing pressure, and we need money to pay the bills.

It's a bit like the prisoner's dilemma[5] but with a different meaning to it.

I think by now you will be starting to see the difference between this book about how to make money and many other books on the subject. Despite being a salesman, I don't want to sell you a dream, but what you bought is a concentrate of realism and pragmatism that, in due time, will lead you somewhere rewarding.

The very first step to make money is either to:

- Find a job that pays more than you spend
- Keep your job if you've already got one and potentially improve on it

It's as simple as that!

Now, are you doing that? Are you looking hard for a job? Does your job pay enough? Do you add enough value? How can you use your job to learn more? Are you focusing enough on your job? Should you change your job?

Find a job

Finding a job is a job in itself: you need to write a good CV, have it proofread by someone you trust or even pay for a professional to do it, apply to jobs online, compile a list of businesses that could be interested in your profile, network on LinkedIn, attend events, get ready for interviews, do the interviews, get the job and keep the job.

<u>Beggars can't be choosers</u>

If you're in a desperate situation, ANY job will do (really anything will do).

For example, me and my wife like to apply the 'survivalist mentality' at all times. So, when my wife lost her job in June 2020, she looked for another one straight away and accepted one with long night shifts EVEN THOUGH we didn't really need the money. Crazy, eh? But would you really want to stop the flow of cash into the coffers when going into a global recession? Obviously, the day after getting that

---

[5] The **prisoner's dilemma** is a paradox in decision analysis in which two individuals acting in their own self-interests do not produce the optimal outcome. (From Investopedia.com).

job she began looking for another job and she got one, with much better conditions, one month later.

Keep the cash coming in, ALL THE TIME.
When in doubt, keep the cash rolling in.
You can improve things later starting from a position of strength.

Make money without making a mess and losing opportunities

Having a massive ego and still hoping to, one day, get into politics and gain something more than money, I've always avoided any job that could compromise my dignity, health or reputation. So while I would have no problem doing jobs of any kind, I have always stayed away from anything which could be perceived as immoral, illegal or dangerous, even if as an atheist some options were, in theory, open. In simple terms, I'd never join the army, work as a sex worker or work in a contaminated environment that could increase my risk of getting sick.

People should join these professions only after having exhausted all the other options. This is not from a moral or ethical perspective, but from a purely money-making perspective: we want to keep as many options open as possible.

Moving on, when you look for a job, you want to try and consider a number of things, let's look at them in detail.

Why am I looking for this job?

When I first arrived in London, I had very little money or time to find a job, and so I started to apply to all the local McDonalds, KFC, Burger Kings etc. to earn some cash and pay for food and rent. This was me, in 2010, with a Master's degree in International Relations, five languages, a specialisation in imports and exports, and experience working in China, France, Hong Kong and Italy….and I was still looking for any job, really!

After a few days spent at an internet point applying for jobs with the Ethiopian owner of the shop looking at me, smirking and saying: "Life is hard, isn't it man?", I decided it was urgent to up my game since that smirk really pissed me off and in a bout of pride I decided that:

- I needed to move into a different room where I had internet and a table – and avoid spending £7 a day at that internet shop
- I had to be fast and look for something better

So, within a few days, I moved into a new place and with the joys of a table and an internet connection, I made a list of manufacturing businesses in England and started to send emails with my CV attached. One answered and I ended up working for them for four years and now, ten years later, this company is one of my main suppliers.

It's actually scary to think what life could have been like if I'd been stuck in a London McDonalds rather than moving to a small town in the North of England.

Message

Very often you'll be underestimating yourself; you'll think you're not good enough; you may think your technical/social/language skills aren't enough. In some cases that may be true but if you work hard at them, within six months you can become proficient in many of the tasks required for most jobs.

Should I move abroad? To a big city? To a cool place?

This is not an option easily accessible to everybody but, if you're young and you can, this is definitely an experience you should consider. As mentioned in 'The starting point', let's not fool ourselves: if you're in the European Union, it's quite easy to move to another country thanks to the Freedom of Movement; however, if you're based in India or Russia, that might be more complicated.

Moving abroad can be an interesting experience but also an expensive mistake. In the 2020s, with rising nationalism and protectionism, with American isolationism reaching its peak and with increasing tensions worldwide, can you easily be an international migrant?

I am one and we, international migrants, really want you to join us, however, it might be difficult for some time so don't 'chase the dragon' but make a pragmatic and realistic assessment of what's best for you at this point in your life.

However, if you can move abroad, my suggestion is DO IT, even if it slows you down.

One of my Japanese friends who lives in Northern Ireland has been living abroad since she was eighteen and her survival skills are amazing; she speaks English fluently and, even if she doesn't realise it, she'll be an amazing asset for any company that does business with Japan.

The simple fact of living abroad and immersing oneself in a different culture for years adds value to you as a person. In my case, a mix of English pragmatism (the English do really like to get things done) and Italian polymorphism (bathing in the complexity of life and bureaucracy) is doing me a lot of favours. If I only had one or the other, I wouldn't be able to do many of the things I'm currently doing.

Message

If you can move abroad, do it before you're thirty. If you can't move abroad now, move later if you can, even if you're older than thirty. Basically, every generalisation is wrong, even this one. In any case, try to move, for a period, far away from your 'home' and be the foreigner/outsider, that will thicken your skin, something that you really DO need to make money.

In which sector should I work?

This is one of the recurring myths: the right sector, the right market.

Obviously if you have studied for ten years to become a doctor, you will probably want to be a doctor. The same goes for lawyers, accountants, civil engineers, and so on.

On this point it is particularly important to notice that it is never too late to learn. You might be 26 and without a degree but, by sacrificing four or five years of your life you can get a degree and work in the field you like. Or you might have realised that you studied the wrong thing and you might want to change your career while you work using the knowledge you have acquired.

There's no fixed formula, even if many education systems want us to think otherwise. The only thing there is, however, is the price to pay: if you're twenty-seven and you want to become a Dr. in chemistry, be ready for ten years of study in a critical part of your life. It might be feasible, but is it worth it?

So, with the exception of those people who have a well-defined career path (and, by the way, that is a VERY GOOD way to make money), many of us are stuck with skills/specialisations which might get less and less marketable, or that are very generic or with limited knowledge/skills either from one's own fault (lack of discipline) or external factors (life!).

Every now and then I look around and I think: "Should I learn this? Is this the best sector for the future? There's so much money in that sector, I want some!".

There have been waves of money-making periods: the .com bubble, the social media bubble, the hyper-specialised niches websites, the electric car sector and, lately, the hand sanitiser and face masks sector.

While economic data and statistics are, on average, right (no pun intended), it's difficult to decide *a priori*, which sector is going to make you the most money. So my advice would be:

- Focus on a sector or job that you like (for example, I liked the idea of selling highly technical products internationally).
- Focus on something where you see some money to be made.
- Focus on something that you know you can make.
- Be realistic. Don't not stop dreaming but be realistic.

On this last point: you might want to be a footballer, a Hollywood actor, a computer scientist, a CERN researcher but we need to move in the realm of the feasible. Go for it, try, but if it does not work move quickly to the next challenge.

> "A good general not only sees the way to victory;
> he also knows when victory is impossible."
> (Polybius)

Message

Choose something which is feasible and that you like or that you can do reasonably well. Most things can be learnt.

The Location/Pay/Career Development Conundrum

Where is the job located? How much does it pay? What are the career opportunities?

This is like a three-dimensional matrix where you are trying to find an optimum point. Let's look at some questions:

- <u>For a job that you only do to pay the bills/study</u>
  Would you rather earn £16,000 in London or £16,000 in a small city of 10,000 people with low cost of living?
- <u>For a job which offers good career opportunities in a big city</u>
  Would you rather earn £28,000 in London and have the opportunity of an amazing career progression or £32,000 in a small city of 10,000 people with very little career prospects?
- Would you rather earn £20,000 in your hometown where you can rely on your parents' house or £20,000 in an international city abroad where you have to pay expensive rent?
- Would you rather buy a house early in a small city or wait years before investing in an expensive property in a big city?

We'll talk more about these points later, but you should think carefully about the following points when looking for a job.

Location: many people are generally attracted to big cities because there are "opportunities", however, without a specific focus (industry, sector, institution) big cities can be rather expensive, including sky-high rent, and rather polluted. On the other extreme, small cities can be parochial and there will be some heavy limitations in terms of career development, study and so forth, with some exceptions.

Pay: Yes, as a first job you want to get experience, but you also want to save money and start to create a deposit to buy a house. If a job pays enough to ONLY pay the bills, the food and some other basic necessities, you either have the wrong job (not paying enough) or are in the wrong place (pay too much for rent and food). Either way you are STUCK and you should move quickly out of this situation: you need to save AT LEAST 20% of your income every month.

Career Development: is there scope for career progression in this job? If not, why am I sticking here longer than strictly needed? Should I study something else? How much will I get?

When looking for a job in London in 2010, I soon realised that with my profile I was going to get anything between £18,000 and £22,000, which basically meant to work to simply survive: serfdom.

One night, talking with an Italian guy who was living with me in the same shared accommodation (a room rented out by some of my late grandfather's friends who moved to the UK in the sixties from the south of Italy) he said something along the lines of: "Life in the north is cheap, but people get really bored there". He was thirty-six, working as a waiter and had a Master's degree in accounting so I asked him: "Have you looked for a job there?", his answer was: "Are you crazy? There is nothing there!".

The next day I was targeting businesses in the north of England for positions between £18,000 and £22,000. One month later, I was working as an export salesperson. I was free from the trap of the big city, he was not.

Message

Do what makes sense, not what looks cool or comfortable.

The Location/Pay/Career matrix is very very very important. How many people that you know are stuck with medium-paying jobs in expensive places and cannot save enough money for a mortgage? How many people get an awful lot of money in a small place and have a great life? How many people are stuck in sub-optimal careers for years and years only to be made redundant close to retirement?

There's no simple answer, it's a complex matter and many more factors come into play but, if you're trying to make money, your main worry should be: "How much money have I made (cash or net worth) at the end of the month?". That, my friend, is what really matters together with your personal development. Most of the other things (cool location, cool office, nice cars) are completely irrelevant to the making of money.

You want to make money and generate wealth; you do not want to APPEAR rich and wealthy.

There is a massive difference.

The inertia of the situation

Each situation has an inertia: people don't like change, situations don't like change and things will go through the path of less resistance which is basically staying still. This means that, as you're reading this book, you might be in a SITUATION (work, life, love, study, money) and that situation has an inertia, a **resistance to change**.

This means that, unless you start to **ACTIVELY DO SOMETHING** (polish up your CV, look for new opportunities, look where and if to move), nothing will change and eventually things will fall apart. This is the nature of life and things in general.

All natural systems degenerate when left to themselves.

This also means there will be a **delay** between the time when you start taking action and the time when that action yields a result. So keep this in mind: you might decide today to look for a new job, but it might take you six months, so you better hurry if that's what you're planning to do. Life doesn't last forever.

Keep your job or change it but do not lose it

We're now assuming that at this point in the narration you've moved from being desperately looking for any job to having some sort of income stability. It makes no sense to think about financial independence when we don't know how to pay the bills for the next six months or if we're worried about food, petrol or basic necessities. If you have not yet reached this point, please complete the following exercise before continuing.

Exercise – Find a job (if it applies)

- Register a professional email: name.surname@something.com
- Register on LinkedIn and make a great profile
- Make your CV, maximum two pages, in the format that works in your country
- Ask your friend who is good with these things to check your CV
- Put together a cover letter
- Subscribe to job sites and apply to all the positions for which you are eligible
- Read about interviews, writing emails, answering questions, tests and so on
- If necessary, move to a new city, region, state, country, even continent!

Moving on

At this point there two possibilities, you either:

- Have a job where there is zero career development in which case you go back one step and start either to:
    - Study something new
    - Look for a different job with a career path
- Have a job in which you can learn new skills

The first kind of jobs are what I call "emergency jobs". These are things that we do to pay the bills, buy food and everything else, and basically not to end up homeless. We always need to move away from those jobs as quickly as possible by studying, learning new skills, starting side businesses, or a combination of these.

The second kind of jobs are those where you're always learning something new. For the last ten years I have been in this kind of jobs and I've always made sure that I was using my time as efficiently as possible. For example, as an international salesperson, you can do a number of things to improve yourself while working:

- Make lists of words that you do not know in different languages
- Learn about selling – there are hundreds of good books
- Learn about your products and sector
- Learn about the company and how it functions
- Improve communication skills
- Improve the company marketing and your creative skills

Over the last ten years I've gone through some **learning cycles** such as:

- In the next six months, I want to read at least three thousand pages of French novels
- In the next three months, I will review all HTML, CSS, SEO to improve the company website
- This year, I will focus on industrial processes

This kind of approach can be repeated for ANY job where you get some sort of specialisation. It's your choice to make the most out of it, **learn as much as you can while getting paid**, create value for the company, the society and yourself. Basically, work hard and study hard.

Again, this isn't rocket science, it's not selling dreams, and it's not just theory; it's very practical stuff:

- Find a job to pay the bills

- Find a job that pays the bills and that allows you to learn some specific skills
- **Practice until you become really good at it**

Message

Get a job for the money, then if needed change it for the skills, practice until you become good, make plans for improvement, and if you risk losing a job, change it before you lose it, keeping in mind the location/pay/career matrix: any change should be an improvement.

FIND A JOB AND USE IT TO LEARN AS MUCH AS POSSIBLE

**IT IS THE SPECIFIC APPLIED KNOWLEDGE OF
HOW VALUE IS CREATED IN A SECTOR
THAT WILL ALLOW YOU TO MAKE MONEY**

**KNOW HOW VALUE IS CREATED AT YOUR COMPANY
AND UNDERSTAND WHY CUSTOMERS BUY**

You might not be able to recreate the same business, but if you're working for them, THEY are doing something very right!

Chapter 3 – Willpower, Choices, and the Brain

Willpower

Chapter 2 was supposed to be practical for a very specific reason. As mentioned in the preface, many other books about how to make money, how to get rich, how to start a company etc. are written by people who are far too advanced for us mere mortals to understand and, while some of the concepts are really powerful, without giving a concrete example, without giving some sort of instructions, many concepts feel very abstract – even when they are not.

At the end of the previous chapter I gave you a very good and simple action plan:

- If you do not have a job, find one, with certain characteristics
- If you have a job with certain characteristics, get the most out of it

That is ridiculously simple and yet, many of you will fail in even doing it and the reason is not lack of skills, ability or time, but lack of **willpower and motivation**. For this very reason, many of those books about personal development and getting rich spend hundreds of pages devising methods to motivate the unmotivated and give willpower to those who do not possess it at that point in their life.

If you're looking for motivational speeches and stories in this book, sorry, you're in the wrong place. The world is full of people who, against all odds, have achieved great things. One of my favourites is Malala Yousafzai, a young girl from Pakistan who was shot in the head by the Taliban because she was trying to oppose the ignorance propagated by their ideology, survived and ended up studying in the UK in one of the best universities in the world, all while winning a Nobel Prize.

If a defenceless young girl can achieve so much, what's our excuse not to act on our dreams and aspirations?

Choices

This is the other elephant in the room: **we make choices and choices have consequences**. Again, this is extremely simple.

In a world that is growing more and more complex, many of the things that we can do, get more and more complicated (or at least it seems so). This means you'll need to work slightly harder, be slightly smarter and move quicker than the previous generation if you want to succeed. Many things boil down to choices:

- Will I order a takeaway for £30 or use that £30 to buy food for the whole week?

- Will I study technical French for three hours after work or will I watch Netflix?
- Will I exercise and keep fit or will I lay down on the couch?
- Will you start talking with more customers or will you send more emails?
- Will you have a hard look at what Google Analytics is saying about your website or will you just assume things?
- Will you re-write that brochure or will you leave it as it is?
- Will you enter a stable relationship with the person you love or will you look for endless fun?

People – we – make choices and most of the time we know what the **financial consequences of those choices are**. For the kind of wealth I describe in this book, the sum of these choices give an intermediate result over the medium-term which, in turn, tends to define what happens in the long-term.

Let me give you two quick examples from two people I know, that show how much difference basic choices can make when repeated over and over.

Story 1

A very clever person and good friend of mine, after some personal struggles, decided that, after the Baccalaureate she wanted to move abroad with her boyfriend and pursue a career in a very specific field. They both decided to do this together, to be loyal to each other and work together to make things happen.

After the Baccalaureate, while most of us at the university were still dreaming of working at the UN, she worked extremely hard to get into the best university in the capital of one of the central countries in Europe with her boyfriend. They both got Master's degrees in some highly specialised fields and started their career young, fresh and well paid.

After this amazing success, this couple stuck together going through many ups and downs, saving money, investing in properties, and continuing their highly specialised jobs. Always remaining very professional in their work and very honest with each other. At the time of writing, they're in their mid-thirties and God knows how much money they have in their bank account – easily more than £2,000,000 and certainly enough to stop working if they wanted to.

We all had their opportunities, but we didn't want to be realistic while at university. Many people who, like them, made money relatively early then let the money drag them down in infidelity and vice, but they stayed loyal to each other and kept the expenses down. Some people might have decided to pursue other passions or ideas, but they remained realistic and now they have a lot of money and enjoy the lifestyle that goes with it.

Story 2

Another very clever person I knew decided to specialise in a field where there were very few opportunities. After years spent chasing a useless degree this friend was stuck in a low paying, non-specialised job and resisted many of my exhortations to join my British adventure and look for a real job. Later, after marriage and infidelity, the little money that was earnt was dilapidated into dispute and fights and now, in his forties, this friend is living a very strange life and contemplating going back to live with his elderly parents.

Choices! If you want money, choose money!

The Brain

We all have one. With the internet and computers it has even been extended and its functions have been improved. Just use it and avoid basic mistakes. Some people – unable to manage their personal past, their instincts, their greed, their slothfulness, their irrational fears, their image of themselves – WASTE their brain, make stupid choices, and never make any money.

To those who have walked on the path to wealth through hard work, dedication and consistency, these situations where people make strange choices can be difficult to understand: many wealthy people made choices so long ago that they've even forgotten them!

Exercise – Your choices

Make a list of the wrong choices you have made and make a list of the wrong choices you were going to make before reading this chapter:

1)
2)
3)
4)

Now write down:

1) What could you stop doing that is currently preventing you from making money?

2) What could you learn to make you more specialised in your field?

3) What could you do this month that could improve your life now and in the future?

Conclusion

This chapter is short on purpose. It contains everything that you need and nothing that you don't. You might want to stop and think about this or read more, but I want to get down to the practicalities of money in this book, so I leave the joys of motivational speeches to others.

Reflect on what you can improve in your personal life, your work, your study. Get a notepad and start writing down all the things you've written down in this book up to this point and call it 'The Money Notepad' and keep it with you at all times.

Chapter 4 – The case for saving and investing

At this point I will assume you are now at peace with yourself and with a world that you're now observing as an external spectator. You're also aware you need to find, keep and improve your job, and use a lot of your time to hone some specific skills that will help you to add value to the company you work for. Finally, I will also assume that you agree with the fact there are some choices that lead to financial wealth while some others will lead to financial disaster and, often, they're interconnected with your personal life, for the best and for the worst.

The richest dad in Babylon

'The richest man in Babylon' by Og Mandino, was one of the first books of the kind I read some years back. The whole book gives simple advice: **save money**. It's so obvious and yet so many people fail to do that for one reason or another. If I remember correctly, in the book the suggestion was to save around 20% of your income each month and, rather than talking about saving, the author talked about: "Paying yourself first, before you pay anybody else".

The idea is that every month you pay your bills, your rent, your food, your other basic necessities, and what you are really doing is paying other people. Og Mandino suggests that, before you pay anybody else, you pay yourself and then you pay the others. This will force you to think creatively to get more money, negotiate harder, improve your finances and so forth.

I think of this book as a mind trick: if you open a separate bank account where, by direct debit or standing order, you automatically pay 20% of your salary into it, eventually you will have enough money to invest. **Once you invest, gradually, your money starts to work for you rather than you working for your money.** Amazingly simple stuff that many people do not see, do, or act upon.

Every month, more than 50% of my income goes into savings and investments, so 20% is a starting point and if it's two of you 20% is really the bare minimum.

The second book I read was **'Rich dad, poor dad'** where the author explained the difference between assets and liabilities:

- **An asset** is something that PUTS MONEY IN YOUR POCKET
- **A liability** is something that TAKES MONEY FROM YOUR POCKET

Simply put, if you have a bank account that pays interests above inflation that is an asset, if you take out a loan with a high interest rate that is a liability. If you invest in a house that gives you rental income that is an asset, if instead you get an expensive car that uses a lot of petrol that is a liability. If you buy shares in a growing company that is an asset, if you buy shares in a dysfunctional company that is a liability. If you buy some tools for your trade that is an asset, if you buy an expensive subscription for entertainment that is a liability.

Wealthy people accumulate assets and keep the liabilities as low as possible.

By putting these two books together, you get the title of this section 'The richest dad in Babylon'. I strongly suggest reading those two books since the examples and the explanations are both fascinating and inspiring.

This means that, after you, and potentially also your partner, have got a job which fits well within the Location/Pay/Career matrix, and you're in specialised jobs, the next step is to save as much as possible and as quickly as possible to be able to INVEST.

But let's work through some numbers to give you a feeling of the power of these concepts when put into practice consistently over the medium-term (around five years).

NOTICE: EVERYTHING TO THIS POINT IS PERFECTLY FEASIBLE

Xiaohui and Jenny

Here I'll tell you, in a practical fashion, the story of Xiaohui and Jenny, a couple who, on the surface, had an easy life and made good money and investments. Let's start with the numbers:

- Xiaohui earns £1,500, and his wife, Jenny, earns £1,600 every month.
- They pay around £700 in rent every month.
- They save £620 every month into a separate account, which means that they save £7,440 every year.
- After three years they have saved £22,320 (£7,440 x 3) which gives them around 20% deposit that they need for their first house which costs around £100,000.
- After buying their house on a £80,000 mortgage with a 2.6% interest rate and a term of 15 years, they start paying £537 per month in mortgage repayment (more than £150 down from their rent of £700).
- Now they can also optimise a bit more their energy bills and car insurance.
- After the first two years their mortgage is down to around £71,045 and they have saved another £14,880 which they now might want to reinvest.

A closer look

Before talking about the numbers in depth, we need to consider some important aspects to give a realistic view of the situation.

Firstly, life does NOT usually go so smoothly that a couple, with both partners working, is in work, all the time, for five years in a row. At the same time, Xiaohui and Jenny have always earnt the same salary, despite them both working and studying very hard and being in jobs where they grow more and more specialised.
To keep the flow of the numbers simple for this example, we can assume that those two things cancel each other out: probably by the fifth year Xiaohui and Jenny are both earning in excess of £2,000 each per month, but it's also likely that at least one of them has been jobless for a period of time.

From my experience, these things more than cancel out and Xiaohui and Jenny have probably MUCH MORE money left at the end of the fifth year.

After the purchase of the house, they decided to rent out a room at around £300 per month, to help pay for the bills and to "make their money work for them". After five years, Xiaohui and Jenny were starting to plan a family and had also invested in a rental property, as well as their own business.

Also, they have both decided that they were going to use only one car, so they've always found a house near to Xiaohui's work while Jenny got the car for commuting.

Now let us look at the expenditures for Xiaohui and Jenny.

Money in (£)		Money out (£)	
Xiaohui wage	1,500	Rent	700
Jenny wage	1,600	Savings – paid into the account	620
		Gas/electricity	100
From the 3rd year (tenant)	300	Council tax	120
		Internet	30
		Phone Xiaohui	12
		Phone Jenny	12
		Car finance	230
		Car insurance	60
		Petrol	100
		Food	250
		Eating out	200
		Emergencies	200
		Various misc.	100
Total in	3,100	Total out	2,734

From these numbers we can see that, even allowing for £200 to eat out (£50 a week) and £300 for emergencies/miscellaneous (could include a holiday fund), Xiaohui and Jenny can still save £366 every month, on top of the £620 that goes into the joint account.

And the end of the third year they bought a house for £100,000 and the numbers are:

- Standard savings: £620 x 12 months x 3 years = £22,320
- Other savings: £366 x 12 months x 3 years = £13,176
- Total savings = £22,320 + £13,176 = £36,000 (approx.)

£36,000 - £20,000 (deposit) - £3,000 (transactions, legal fees) = £13,000

After buying the house at the end of the third year, they were left with around £13,000 in the bank.

From the third to the fifth year their numbers look like:

- Savings left after house purchase: £13,000
- Standard savings: £620 x 12 months x 2 years = £14,880
- Other savings: £366 x 12 months x 2 years = £8,784
- Room rental: £300 x 12 months x 2 = £7,200
- Total savings = £43,000 (around)

Also, we shouldn't forget that:

- House bought for: £100,000
- Equity in the house after 2 years: around £70,000 (they've already repaid around £10,000 of the mortgage)
- Value of the house (assuming a slowly growing market): £105,000
- Net worth of Xiaohui and Jenny
    - £43,000 in savings
    - £35,000 in equity
    - Total: £78,000+

From this base, Xiaohui and Jenny can now decide whether to almost close off their mortgage, invest in a property, or do something else with their money.

Exercise – Know your numbers

I want you to spend some time using Excel or pen and paper to work through YOUR OWN numbers. If you have just thought: "I don't know how to use Excel", well close the book and follow a quick online course.

You need to know your own numbers and specifically look for these things:

- How much are you earning?
- How much are you spending?
- How much are you saving?
- How much could you save in one, two, five years?
- What is the average house price in your area?
- How much will you need for a deposit for a house?
- What is the mortgage repayment going to be if you do a twenty-five year mortgage?
- How much can you rent a room for in your house?

If you Google things like:

- Property for sale (in the UK the main website in Rightmove)
- Mortgage calculator
- Mortgage finder
- Room rent cost

You can find all the tools you need to do a quick forecast and get an idea of how much you could save and how much your net worth could be in one, two or five years.

DO THE EXERCISE,
OTHERWISE YOU DO NOT KNOW WHERE YOU STAND

Exercise – A separate savings account

Tomorrow, go to your bank and open a separate bank account where money is paid in every month. If you're a couple, open a joint bank account where you put your savings. The money should come out of your main account into the saving account on the first of every month, as soon as you get paid and you should NEVER use them unless for a real investment (i.e. ASSETS), not for holidays, not for emergencies, not for shopping, not for self-justified fake investments (you do NOT need that £300 microphone!).

Open a separate bank account and start pouring as much cash as possible in it.

Message

These simple numbers should really be eye-opening for many young people.

When I was growing up, what I really missed was someone to explain these numbers to me in plain and simple terms and tell me: "Look, find love, find a job, become good at what you do, save money, buy a house, rent a room, pay off the mortgage, invest and start your own business". It's as simple as that and you don't need a degree in anything special to follow these rules.

Obviously, the more you get paid the quicker you can save money, and a degree or some technical education is helpful, however, it is **the principle which is important** and many people cannot see this clearly.

Often, the desire for money is a general desire which is not followed up by a specific plan. This is probably the first and easiest plan that you need: **a plan to buy your first house,** which, in time, might become part of your portfolio that generates some income.

Save some more money - NOW!

Since you have invested in this book, which will make you A LOT of money, let me help you to save some money now. You're probably haemorrhaging money this very moment, so let us STOP this now.

Take some time to do these things:

- Delete all the non-essential subscriptions that you have (check for penalties)
- Check if you can save money on gas, electricity, internet, mobile, car insurance (check every year)
- Decide that you will NOT spend money on unnecessary things
- Look for coins, paper money, money lost on ancient bank accounts, and put it all in your newly created bank account
- Pay off any debt where you're paying interest – interest is a sin, repent!

Now, doing the above is much more important than continuing to read. So now, I really do mean NOW, close the book and go and make some money by SAVING some money and optimising your expenses. By doing this, you'll probably recover the cost of this book ten to one hundred times within the coming weeks and months. This is a massive return on investment. It's boring but, would you do something boring for two hours if it paid £600 pounds per year? Definitely YES.

A worked example for one person

In order not to demoralise singles, I provide here a worked example for one person to show what can be achieved following these principles.

Let's do some calculations together. I will demonstrate a very simple example and it's important that you learn to think in these terms. If there are any magic tricks to make money, this is one of them: knowing your numbers, thinking about them, **looking how to improve them** and learning to make a forecast.

In this story our friend Xiaohui didn't meet Jenny but he still wanted to make money. Also, he didn't go to the university and started to work when he was eighteen years old on almost minimum wage but in a job where he could always learn something and improve.

His monthly IN/OUT table looked like this

Year 1

Money in (£)		Money out (£)	
Xiaohui wage	1,000	Rent (room in shared house)	300
		Food	200
		Mobile phone contract	10
		Going out	90
		Miscellaneous	100
Total in	**1,000**	**Total out**	**700**

Savings per month: £300. Savings in the first year: £3,600.

During the first year, Xiaohui was busy learning everything he could about his job and got a pay rise the following year.

Year 2

Money in (£)		Money out (£)	
Xiaohui wage	1,300	Rent (room in shared house)	300
		Food	200
		Mobile phone contract	10
		Going out	90
		Miscellaneous	100
Total in	**1,300**	**Total out**	**700**

Savings per month: £600. Savings in the second year: £7,200.

By the end of the second year Xiaohui has already got £7,200 + £3,600 = £10,800 in his bank account. He's still single and is now so good at his job that he will either get another pay rise or, more likely, move to a new and better paid job in a cheaper area.

Year 3

Money in (£)		Money out (£)	
Xiaohui wage	1,500	Rent (room in shared house)	300
		Food	200
		Mobile phone contract	10
		Going out	150
		Miscellaneous	200
Total in	**1,500**	**Total out**	**860**

Savings per month: £640. Savings in the third year: £7,680.

Total savings in the third year = £18,480 (£10,800 + £7,680).

At the end of the third year, Xiaohui, has been able to save around £18,000. He has also spent more money during the third year, but he stuck to his plan and didn't buy a car, spent very little money on luxuries (such as holidays), and focussed all his efforts into saving money. These have been three very hard years and while other people, paid by their parents, were enjoying the university life, Xiaohui was saving almost £20,000 and getting three years of work experience while also studying by himself.

At this point, Xiaohui decides to buy a house. He looks around and sees that he can buy a small house for around £60,000 in that area. He actually moved there for this specific reason: he wanted to invest in properties.

So, at the beginning of the fourth year, Xiaohui puts down a £10,000 deposit, pays £3,000 in legal fees and on some basic household items, and is left with:

- £5,000 in the bank
- £50,000 mortgage

With it being his first house, he thought he'd play it safe so he decided to pay the mortgage over twenty years which, with interest rates at 2.2% means a repayment of £258 per month. So, let's look at the fourth year. He also started to rent out the second bedroom in his house to help with the expenses.

Year 4

Money in (£)		Money out (£)	
Xiaohui wage	1,500	Mortgage	260
Room rental	300	Gas/electricity	100
		Council tax	100
		Internet	30
		Mobile phone contract	10
		Food	200
		Going out	150
		Miscellaneous	200
Total in	**1,800**	**Total out**	**1,050**

Savings per month: £750. Savings in the fourth year: £9,000.

Total savings in the year = £9,000 + £5,000 from the previous year = £14,000. Mortgage left to pay after one year (£48,000), which is a net gain of £2,000. Value of the house after some work and improvement: £62,000.

This means that Xiaohui is now twenty-two years old and finds himself in this position:

- He really knows his job and is looking for a promotion
- He has a house that's starting to bring him some rental income
- He has an equity in the house of around £14,000 (£62,000 - £48,000)
- He has around £14,000 in savings
- His net worth is approaching £30,000 and is growing very fast

Let's see what happens in the fifth year:

Year 5

Money in (£)		Money out (£)	
Xiaohui wage	1,700	Mortgage	260
Room rental	300	Gas/electricity	100
		Council tax	100
		Internet	30
		Mobile phone contract	10
		Food	200
		Going out	150
		Miscellaneous	200
Total in	**2,000**	**Total out**	**1,050**

Savings per month: £950. Savings in the fifth year: £11,400.

Total savings to the year = £14,000 + £11,400 = £25,400.
Mortgage left to pay after two years (£46,000), which is a net gain of £4,000.
Value of the house after some work and improvement: £65,000.

This means that Xiaohui is now twenty-three and finds himself in this position:

- He is a professional in his job
- He has a house that has already brought some good rental income
- He has an equity in the house of around £19,000 (£65,000 - £46,000)
- He has around £25,400 in savings
- His net worth is approaching £45,000 and is growing very fast

As you can see, Xiaohui alone, by following this really cruel logic and starting from zero (no inheritance, no special education, no partner) has been able to establish himself. At this point, he might now decide to reduce his mortgage from £46,000 to £26,000 (pay £20,000 from his savings) and this would leave him with basically £6,000 in the bank and probably another two years before being mortgage free by his twenty-fifth birthday.

Final considerations

Before moving onto the next chapter, try to work out your own numbers, see where you are now and where you could get just by doing the right things in five years. It won't take you long and will give you either a motivation boost to save more or it will expose an unsustainable situation you need to get out of as quickly as possible. Since the first house is an important step after your job, the next chapter will try to highlight some important points and concepts.

Chapter 5 – The First House

It would be unfair if I didn't spend some more time on this topic: the first house. Once you've bought your first house, the second, third and fourth comes easier. But if you screw up your first house, then this could lead to disaster or slow you down for years and years. Buyer beware!

Once I came across a book which was quite heavy to read but had some genuine pearls of wisdom: 'The Millionaire Real Estate Investor'. The book itself contained really all the information you need to become a Millionaire Real Estate Investor, however, as many other books of this kind, it started with some assumptions that are not always valid. In the coming pages, I will use some of the knowledge I have acquired from that book but also add my own perspective.

Why you should invest in a property

When you buy a house you usually make a sound investment because:

- You stop paying rent to a landlord - generally higher than a mortgage
- You repay your mortgage and part of those repayments increase your net worth
- If you must move away from the area you can rent the house out or you can sell it
- House value usually increases in the long term[6]
- Rent prices usually increase in the long-term
- You can easily optimise various bills
- You get more stability, better credit rating, better offers
- You can rent out a room in your own house and make some money
- You can use your house as the base for your business

With all these positives for buying a house, it is really a mystery to me why people are so hesitant to invest in properties. Buying your first house, **when done well**, is the single most important step to financial independence.

Many people worry about Forex trading, stock market and cryptocurrencies while paying their landlords' mortgages and making them wealthier. It really is mind blowing but, to be honest, it's not a mystery since I know exactly what stops people from buying their first house:

---

[6] This is not an absolute truth; it depends on demographics. Do some research into the property market in your country and see if the population is forecast to increase and by how much over the next thirty years. And then ask yourself: "Will enough houses be built?"

THE FEAR OF COMMITMENT

- If I buy this house with my partner then I'm committed forever
    - Wrong, you can buy at 50% each, and if you split up, you can either sell it, rent it out and split the profit, or one of you could buy the other out
- If I buy a house here, then I cannot move away until I pay it off
    - Wrong, you can sell it or, even better, rent it out
- If I buy a house in this city, I am stuck with my current employer
    - Wrong, you can sell it or, even better, rent it out
- What if I cannot pay the mortgage?
    - What if you cannot pay your landlord?
      At least with a house you own you can rent one or two rooms; it takes longer for banks to evict you; you can always rent it out totally; the mortgage is likely to be lower than your rent and should always be lower than what you can rent it out for!
- What if house prices crash?
    - Who cares? You're not buying to sell in the short-term (or even ever) but to create a long-term investment
- What if interest rates go up?
    - You can have a fixed term mortgage for five or even ten years and you'll always pay the same amount
- What if the house sets on fire?
    - Pay for insurance

It's extremely easy to see that those are all irrational fears in most cases, in most markets, in most times.

Unless you live in a country where there are high levels of political instability (Venezuela), negative population growth (Bulgaria), a risk of war or something extreme (Syria, Libya), you should consider investing in real estate and land: the world population will increase in the coming decades from seven billion to ten billion.

Why on earth haven't you bought a house yet?
Because you haven't rationally analysed this very important first step.

Message

In most cases, unless you're quite sure that you will be jobless and broke for months and months within the next half a year, all the fears about buying a house are irrational.

Do INVEST in the first property
Do NOT buy your first home

Here's the point where most people screw up, so please focus.

After years and years of saving 20% of their income, finally Pedro and Vivienne (who are they?) had enough for a deposit and they bought the home of their dreams, with a magnificent garden, three bedrooms and triple-glazed windows in an established neighbourhood with a very good school and local amenities. They could only put a 5% deposit on the £400,000 house, but it was an amazing house, bought at top price, and with a thirty-five year mortgage. But you should have seen the garden! Unfortunately, the following year the market crashed, they had no savings after the holiday to the Maldives, lost their jobs and eventually sold the house at a loss. They were back to square one.

This is not a rare story of self-inflicted financial pain and again, it's amazing how many people do this.

After years of saving, some people buy their first house not as an investment or even as a home, but as a status symbol: I got this amazing house, in this good area, so I am a worthy person. Obviously, for any rational observer, this is pure folly and an example that must be avoided at all costs.

On the other hand, let us look again at the story of Xiaohui and Jenny.

They bought their first house keeping in mind these principles:

- The house should be at walking distance from the workplace(s)
- This saves money and insurance on a second car/transportation
- It must not be too expensive and WELL WITHIN the repayment capabilities
- Ideally a second room to rent out for extra income would not hurt
- The area should be safe and well-connected, but no need to be glamourous
- Well-connected for access to train lines in case one of the two loses a job
- Easy to rent out if they decided to move away
- The potential rent should be more than the value of the fixed mortgage (at least 125%)
- Five years fixed mortgage that allows overpayments of 10%
- The house should be well-built and easy to maintain

The main difference between Pedro and Vivienne and Xiaohui and Jenny was that the first were looking to buy a status symbol, a glamorous home, and weren't ready to compromise, the second instead were making an investment in order to make money in the medium-long term.

**Be an investor, not a consumer.
Buy assets that put money in your pockets,
do not buy liabilities that take money out of your pockets.
Buy rationally and justify emotionally later, not the contrary.**

When buying a house you really want to do a lot of research, you need to look for similar houses in the same area, find those that have been recently listed, talk and make friends with the estate agents and explain to them your needs, explain to them that you're looking to buy something below market value (ideally you want a 20% discount), investigate the crime in the area, walk in that neighbourhood at night, look for any infrastructural development, check for flooding, earthquakes, mining, subsidence, debts secured against the house, access to motorways and railways, nearby universities, price of the rooms to rent out and so on.

Basically, you need to spend dozens of hours understanding the housing market in that specific area so that, after a few months of research, many viewings, many hours spent talking with estate agents and neighbours, once the opportunity comes, **you go and get it straight away, at the right price**.

Luck = Preparation x Opportunity

Message

The first two, or even, three properties that you buy should be an investment. Don't worry too much about what you like, just make sure it's a sound investment, that can more than pay for itself if you need to move away and rent or sell. Make the numbers work so that you can pay the mortgage even in the worst-case scenario. Then pay it off quickly and move onto the next investment.

<u>Exercise – Start to look for your first house</u>

Visit a property website and start to look for properties at a commutable distance from your work which:

- You can have a deposit for (now or within two or three years maximum)
- Are in decent areas where you won't have problems with crime
- You could afford by not paying more than 25% of your salary on a twenty-five year mortgage
- Have at least two bedrooms – one to rent out
- You could rent out at a higher price than the mortgage
- Ideally is at walking distance from your job if you don't have a car and if you're planning to stay there for two or more years

If you find that such a property does not exist, then it means that you're either earning or saving too little or living in an expensive city. So, the Location/Pay/Career

Development matrix might need to be reassessed unless there's a strong reason to stay put.

The importance of criteria

Some books spend hundreds of pages saying the same things. Here I am giving you all the essence, but these points are so important that I will repeat them.

It is extremely important to stick to some specific criteria:

- Kind of area: not too good, not too bad. It is in these 'frontier areas' where you can really make a good deal.
- Kind of house: easy to rent out, good rental yield
- Number of rooms: minimum two, with one to rent out
- Location: strategically located for job resilience
- Location: avoid the need for a second car
- Estate agents: you need to talk with them
- Purchasing price: **needs to be lower than the asking price (you can negotiate!)**
- **Mortgage** repayments: well within your means
- Timing: ideally you want to **"buy when there's blood on the streets even if it's your own"**

On this last point, one of the houses we bought was purchased two weeks after the Brexit referendum, when the country wanted to kick Europeans (me and my wife) out of the UK and the market was panicking. That resulted in a 15% discount on the price that we paid.

Also, remember that the perfect house does not exist, what exists is the right house at the right price. When looking for a house, if it's legal in your country, you should make a number of offers to different houses at the price you think is a fair deal: whoever accepts gets your money and you get the right house at the right price.

Another important criterion is the mortgage. My strong suggestion is to get a mortgage broker but shop around. Some charge a fortune and some are more honest and will give you a reasonable price (i.e. why pay £500 when you can pay £150?).

I found that a good mortgage broker can make the whole process much smoother, offer advice, and get you better interest rates.

Once you have a mortgage broker, you need to play with the numbers and decide these five things:

- How much do you want to pay monthly?
  Personally, given the financial crisis of 2008, the recession of 2010, Brexit, wars and Coronavirus, I have always opted for very LOW monthly repayments. The least I have paid on a mortgage was £182 per month and the most was £537. My assumption is that if I can, I will overpay 10% of the mortgage, but if I cannot I will not have to! This, however, means that you're paying more interest, so overpayments are practically a must.

- Repayment or interest only?
  I always like to go for repayments since the final plan is not to sell the house (which will have increased in value) but to keep it as an investment

- Fixed or variable rate? If fixed for how long?
  Again, I have always preferred some certainty, so a fixed rate makes you sleep better at night. The dilemma here is: "How long should you fix it for?". If you fix it for a period which is too long, you end up paying a lot of interest and are stuck with a mortgage provider; moreover, you would incur penalties if you wanted to close the mortgage earlier. If you fix it for a short period of time, then you need to re-negotiate the mortgage after a while, which has its own associated costs. I'd recommend going for around two to five years.

- Overpayments permitted?
  This is a must.

- Other terms and conditions
  Ideally you want a mortgage with no fees, especially if you're planning to change provider after a few years.

By playing with these criteria, doing your research, buying at the right time, in the right place, at the right price, and then committing at least a year of your life to live in that house while renting a room out, it's very difficult to go wrong.

Some final points

This chapter doesn't not seek to be a substitute for reading and researching - this is more of a starting point to give you some of the mental tools (the bookshelves) where you can put additional information. There are hundreds of articles on the internet on this topic.

Property markets change from country to country, from city to city. Some of the things that I have explained here are harder to achieve in some other countries where lending requirements are stricter than in the UK (for example Italy and France), but some points are valid everywhere.

In some countries, banks will allow you to rent out a room, in some others they might not; in some places you might need a stable permanent contract before getting a mortgage, in some others you might just need three months' worth of payslips; in some regions location is very important, in some other regions the difference is not so much.

In any case, when I've applied these criteria to potential investments in England, Italy, France and Spain, they worked out well. When I applied these to places like India…well, miracles can happen since the economy is growing so fast. But then, you can only do that if you're Indian or living there on a permanent basis.

Finally, during the course of this book we'll look again at many of these topics with ever greater depth, but my advice is: start doing your research now. I don't want to spoon-feed you with all the different kinds of mortgages available, with how interest rates work and so on.

You can find this information online very easily. Certainly, later in the book we'll talk more about this but you really DO NEED to do your research now: you will not develop a certain way of thinking by going through this book all at once, so here is an exercise.

Exercise

Find out the following information:
- What kinds of mortgages are there in your country?
- What are the lending requirements?
- How much deposit do you need?
- How much do mortgage brokers charge?
- Which are the best banks?
- What is the interest rate now?
- What are the best websites to search for houses?
- Who are some good estate agents?
- What is the average price for a 'starter home' in your area of interest?
- How long will it take you to get a deposit together?

Please spend a few hours educating yourself before moving onto the next chapter. Making money is an active process, so go and MAKE something.

Chapter 6 – Preparing to go Beyond

Before proceeding past this point it's important to realise one thing. You might have been reading this book for a few hours, however, the path that has been described here easily takes a few years to implement. You might now be considering looking for a new job, or whether I've got a point when I say that fears of buying a house are mainly irrational.

What you shouldn't forget, is that between the moment when you start to think about any of those things and the moment when they happen, months, or even years, are likely to pass.

The real difficulty, however, is not so much in the implementation *per se* of what you have just read but it has more to do with the choices, the self-control, self-restraint and rational application of logic to things that can involve you quite emotionally (buying a home vs investing in a property).

For this reason, I would strongly suggest you keep this book with you, almost as a reminder, and review each chapter as you progress toward real financial independence.

Recap

We first opened up our minds and made sure that the idea of continuous learning and continuous improvement are agreed on (remember the bookshelves) but also the need to manage the noise, the stimulus and the response. We discussed the circle of concern and influence and how we need to focus on our actions rather than worrying about things we cannot control.

We then discussed why it's important to find a job to pay the bills and then a job that puts you on a road of continuous improvement. **This is extremely important** because your skills can improve over time, so will your employability, your capability to generate value for the company you work for, and eventually, for your own company.

Then we explained why many people fail in attaining even a basic level of wealth. We found the causes to be mainly rooted in the lack of willpower, in crazy choices or in the conscious choice of not using one's brain.

In Chapter 4, I emphasised the power of saving and investing, talking about 'The richest dad in Babylon' and the couple, Xiaohui and Jenny. We then delved into how to buy your first house, how to buy it well, and how to think about this first property as an investment.

If you've followed these steps, you should be in the following situation:

- You and your partner have decided to live and make money together
- You've probably developed some sort of personal development program, perhaps you have moved abroad, or somewhere where the cost of living is cheaper in comparison with the salaries
- You're both working in jobs that pay a decent wage and allow you to save enough money each month and always learn something new
- You've studied the local area thoroughly and made a first property investment where you are now living
- Ideally, you also have a friendly tenant, who is helping you to pay the bills
- And you've saved some money in the bank

Well done! Level 1 completed…so, what's next?

NOTICE: EVERYTHING TO THIS POINT IS PERFECTLY FEASIBLE

Between Level 1 and Level 2

After years of drudgery, you're finally there: you and your partner have got a house and paid for a portion of it, paid jobs, some money in the bank... and what do you do? Really, what do you do in this golden position?

You fuck up!
This is what you do.

Don't worry, we've all been there. Sometimes it's the inexperience, sometimes it's the price you pay for sanity after being stuck in the rat race for years, sometimes it's just the desire for adventure. Most of us, willingly or unwillingly, once we find ourselves with too much time, power, money, freedom, we mess up because we don't know how to handle it.

Obviously "destruction leads to a very rough road, but it also breeds creation"[7] so even those mistakes make part of our development and making mistakes is key to our growth.

Niels Bohr said:

"An expert is a person who has made all the mistakes that can be made in a very narrow field."

In the case of me and my partner, we left our jobs at the same time, went on a holi-

---

[7] From Californication

day to Thailand and Singapore, came back, half-heartedly and without any industry experience started a web design company and, within a few months, were running out of money and ended up renting out our own home and working for two years in positions we did not like. Basically, three or four months of freedom cost us two and a half years of a miserable life while we were trying to keep everything together.

On the bright side, I grew professionally and my wage increased, we bought our second house in a depressing but easily rentable sad place, met some good friends and started to really understand the logic behind investment in property but also behind starting a successful business.

Message

Between a hypothetical Level 1 and an undefined Level 2, there's a strong possibility you'll make big mistakes. Stop and don't do it, even if you really really really want to. If it's working, if it's bringing money in, keep it going and work on the side, go on holidays, spend more money on takeaways, spend money on something you like, take it slower but don't ever ever ever break any system that is bringing you money unless you've already replaced it with another one.

Always keep the money rolling in, unless you have proof that a change can bring in more money (selling the first house and making a lot of profit, a new signed contract for a job not too far away, money in the bank coming from side activities etc.).

Level 2

Now, the actual formation of Level 2 will really depend on your personal circumstances and I cannot say: "this is what you should do". What I can do, however, is share some of my experiences and then you can come to your own conclusions. The important point is that you **do not break any mechanism that is bringing you money**.

Option 1: Buy a second property

If the situation makes sense and this is something that you would like to do, invest in a second property. As with the first, this process will take weeks or even months, you'll need to do your research, you'll also need a bigger deposit unless you decide to buy this second property and change your main property into a buy-to-let. Whatever you decide to make just be aware that from the moment you own a second property you will:

- Make more money and potentially attract more taxes
- Have to file tax returns
- Have to deal with tenants and legal requirements
- Have more work to do in general for little returns for the first few years

The joy of property investment is that anyone can do it; the damnation of it is also that anyone can do it.

Option 2: Start a side business

We will explore this in more detail later in the book, however this is also an option you can follow on one condition: you should not use the money you have saved to invest in your business. Some money (£1,000-£3,000) is ok, but more than that means that there's a problem with your business model. We'll look at this later, as certain chapters are dedicated to how to build a business from the ground up.

Another condition of this is that you do this in your OWN FREE TIME, and it should not interfere in any way with your full-time job. Finally, you really want to start a business in a sector where you have had direct commercial experience: you don't want to pay for another learning curve, **you want to recycle some knowledge, contacts and processes**.

This also means that even if you're passionate about something, it's not a viable option if you don't have any real industrial experience, so the first step will be Option 3.

Option 3: Start working on a second job to further your knowledge of a sector you like

Imagine that you can get paid to learn something you're interested in, amazing isn't it? Well, that is simply a job you like. For some things this could be easier (guitar or language classes), for some things it can be more complicated (CAD modelling, fluid dynamics). If you look hard enough on freelancer websites and so on, you can find work in the field of your interest, develop experience and then use that experience to open your own SIDE business, all while getting paid. You might also consider working on weekends and evenings, if your current job allows it.

Option 4: Invest in financial products, pensions etc.

I'm not usually very keen on these, simply because I haven't spent enough time learning about them, because of the intrinsically greedy nature of humans, coupled with the reward structure for taking risks for some managers and the simple fact that I don't want other people to manage my money. However, this is an option too, but make sure you read the small print.

Option 5: Invest in specialised education

You can invest time and money into improving your education, however, make sure it's a realistic objective. If you're working eight hours per day and commuting another one or two hours, can you really study five hours a day for the next three years?

Message

Basically, you either start investing in real estate, working on your own business, investing in financial products, or in specialised education. The choice is yours but be realistic.

***

We're now getting ready to move to Level 2, however, there are a number of things we need to get right before moving on to invest in more properties or start a side business.

Exercise – What are your options

Take again pen and paper and write down your options, analyse them, think about what can bring you more money, what activities you could do, what you could get paid, how much more money you would get with further education and so on.

Put your standard finances in order

- Are you paying interest on any credit cards?
- How long have you been with your gas/electricity supplier? Can you get a better deal?
- Do you need internet, phone and TV or can you do with internet alone?
- How much do you pay per month for your mobile? Do you really need that much data?
- Do you need an expensive gym subscription? Can't you run at the park? Do yoga at home?
- Are you still paying for your bank account? Can you get a better deal somewhere else?
- Have you overpaid your mortgage? Is it going down as fast as you can?
- What about your car insurance? Can you improve on that?
- Have you got a life/sickness insurance? It's cheaper if you're young.
- What subscriptions can you cancel? Will you have time to watch Netflix once you're working full-time and on your side business at the same time?
- Can you stock buy some long-life products?
- Can you save some money on your weekly shopping?
- Have you got coins and notes waiting for inflation to eat their value away?
- Is there anything you can sell online that you'll never use again?
- Are you paying an unjustifiably high price for something because of loyalty to a brand?

If you've followed my advice and changed city/country, got a specialised job, worked hard, studied hard, saved money and bought a first house, it's very likely that in the chaos some things have got out of control.

You might have ended up with three sets of pots, two vacuum cleaners, two gym subscriptions, an expensive energy bill, some bad shopping habits, and so on. It's important to really keep control of these things and review everything at least once a year.

Some might think that this approach is a bit *penny-wise and pound-foolish*: "If I'm getting the big things right (job, house, saving) why should I waste my precious time thinking about saving £2 here, £3 there?"

Let's look at a medium-bad scenario reviewing the list above and see how much money you could save **every year** by carrying out those activities. I will base this on my own numbers in the UK in 2020, assuming that I hadn't optimised my finances and had let things get out of control.

Are you paying interests on any credit card?
Yes, let's say that I pay £5 per month on the credit card because I forget to pay it off or I don't have a direct debit set up.
Potential saving: £60

How long have you been with your gas/electricity supplier? Can you get a better deal?
I'd been with them for two years, checked on a comparison website and I could save £200 in a year.
Potential saving: £200

Do you need internet, phone and TV or can you do with internet alone?
I could do with internet alone but I like to have the whole package at £45 per month; the basic package is £20 per month.
Potential saving: £300

How much do you pay per month for your mobile? Do you really need that much data?
I got a contract for £20 a month and unlimited calls, 20 GB of data etc. I rarely use more than 1 GB to be honest. A contract for 2 GB per month and enough calls and texts is around £9 a month.
Potential savings: £132

Do you need an expensive gym subscription? Can't you run at the park? Do yoga at home?
I pay £20 per month for the gym, it's a very good one, but I could do most things from home or at the local park.
Potential savings: £240

Are you still paying for your bank account? Can you get a better deal somewhere else?
Yes, I pay around £5 a month, I know I could switch to a new account but then I need to switch everything else.
Potential savings: £60

Have you overpaid your mortgage? Is it going down as fast as you can?
No, I was planning to overpay the 10% (£7,000) on my outstanding balance but then I thought that I would rather keep the money in the bank and upgrade the garden.
Potential savings (one off): £2,405 (assuming that you have £80,000 left on your mortgage, 13 years and 2.4% interest rate)

What about your car insurance? Can you improve on that?
I have checked quotes and yes, I could save £90 this year
Potential savings: £90

Have you got a life/sickness insurance? It's cheaper if you're young.
This is a cost, however, if you're younger than thirty years old and get a lifetime cover, you can get it very cheaply compared to when you're forty with two kids and you want to give them some security.

What subscriptions can you cancel? Will you have time to watch Netflix once you're working full time and on your side business at the same time?
I pay around £10 per month for Spotify and £10 for Netflix
Potential savings: £240

Can you stock buy some long-life products? Can you save some money on your weekly shopping?
This can be big, you could save hundreds per year, let's put an approximate amount
Potential savings: £300

Have you got coins and notes waiting for inflation to eat their value away?
Potential profit: £50

Is there anything you can sell on eBay or other online marketplaces that you'll never ever use again?
Potential profit: unknown

Are you paying an unjustifiably high price for something because of loyalty to a brand?
Potential savings: £50

Total savings for the year: £1,722
Total savings in five years: £8,610
Total savings (including interest not paid thanks to the overpayment): **£11,015**

Over the course of thirty years this translates roughly into: £11,015 x 6 (5 year periods) = **£66,090,** which is basically the cost of a nice little investment property.
This does not include the fact that, the more money you have, the quicker you pay off the mortgage, the quicker you can invest in another property, the quicker you can pay off the second mortgage and get a real passive income.

Message

Review at least once every six months exactly where your money is going, keep an eye out and make cuts where you can whenever possible.

Sustainability, minimalism, and frugality

Just to be clear, I am not advocating to live a miserable life, this is not the ideal that I'm trying to advocate.

Vincent Van Gogh - The Potato Eaters

However, in the West, but also in Japan, Australia, and in many other parts of the world, we're really living unsustainable lives and spending our hard-earned cash on random stuff that we don't really need. Let me give you some examples.

Your car

Where we live, we simply *need* a car. For the first two years I lived in England, I walked everywhere and those were very windy years of my life. I also ended up spending a lot of money on taxis, in local shops, and on expensive local transport. So, after realising that I was not in London but in a God-forgotten small town, I finally decided to buy a car.

The first car was a big mistake: a used car, from a dodgy garage that stopped working (oil leak in the engine) after a few weeks. There's a saying that goes:

I am not rich enough to buy cheap things!

and that really is true. When it comes to something you need and are planning to use for a long time, you should invest in some level of quality.

After that first expensive lesson, I found a reputable car dealer, traded in this old broken car, and told the car salesman that:

- I needed a reliable car to go from A to B
- That shouldn't cost a lot in maintenance
- With a good warranty
- Reasonable repayment terms
- And a USB port to listen to audiobooks in French and Spanish while driving

The car salesman looked at me asking what colour, speed, model, make etc. I said that I didn't care, what I needed was a tool with certain characteristics to achieve certain results, nothing more nothing less.

Ten minutes later I was signing a form for a car that was going to:

- Cost me £220 per month for the next five years
- Have a lifetime warranty up to 100,000 miles
- Have a 1.4 engine which means lower insurance
- Have five doors to bring family and friends around
- Have 0% interest finance
- Have a USB port
- Be red, since this was the available colour at the time

This was in 2013, and seven years later, the car has helped us with six house moves, 66,000 miles, brought me and my wife, in turns, to different jobs, allowed us to explore the whole of the North of England, Wales, Scotland and it is still running well and under warranty.

During these seven years, at one point I was commuting four hours per day by train/walk to avoid buying a second car; at one point the car had stickers on it with the name of our web-design company that failed; many times it has served as a van to move things from one house to another.

It has never been a problem to repay, never something to go faster than the allowed speed limit, always serviced and treated like an investment, never perceived as a status symbol.
Some other friends, during the same seven years, bought two different cars to "change the model", crashed a car by speeding too much, got a car which cost £550 per month for five years (basically a mortgage) and many other crazy things.

So, generally speaking, you can do many things right in terms of saving money on bills, internet, bank accounts etc. but if you can buy a £12,000 car and you decide to buy a £30,000 one, you are, at least £18,000 worse off, and it does not matter what justification you give to yourself.

Assets and Liabilities: A Review

Among the first concepts introduced in this book were those of assets and liabilities.

- An asset is something that puts money in your pocket.
- A liability is something that takes money from your pocket.

As far as possible, you always want to buy/produce assets and eliminate/reduce liabilities.

If you buy a car for £12,000 and you use that car to go to work, go shopping, go on holidays, move house, or even for your business, that car is clearly an asset. Sure, it's an asset that's losing value (today I could sell this seven-year-old car for £3,500) but it's still an asset.

On the other hand, if you buy a £30,000 car and you use it to do the same things as above and also to go around the city centre trying to impress who knows who and burning fuel, this is a liability for yourself and for the environment.

<u>The house</u>

If you buy a massive house, with many things that can go wrong and a massive long mortgage that will take forever to repay and over which you'll pay a lot of interest, that's clearly a big liability.

If instead you buy a smaller and compact house, with a small mortgage that you pay off in a few years and you rent out one or two rooms, this is still, technically speaking, a liability, but it's a smaller one that has the potential to become an asset.

The computer

This is the interesting one. A few weeks ago I was discussing PCs with my brother, and here you have to strike a balance which is, given the value and the duration of these machines, more of a philosophical exercise than a physical one.

If you're working using some 2D/3D software and your computer was very cheap, you've probably got a massive liability because you're wasting hours and hours every day waiting for the processors to catch up. On the other hand, if you're only writing, answering emails and watching YouTube that's probably an asset. Also, the contrary is true.

Clothing

Yes, indeed, we're getting down to an obscene level of greediness or optimisation, depending on the point of view.

My mother grew up in an era where clothing was quite important, has always been obsessed with "what other people might think and say". More than her specific character, it's a trait of southern Italians. In fact, if you go to any city centre there, very often it's like a fashion show with many people dressed up as if they were going somewhere very important.

I've always perceived this as a waste of time and money:

- If you need to go somewhere important THEN you dress accordingly
- Otherwise, relax

However, travelling around I realised that this is more common than I thought. In the middle of India, surrounded by rubbish, you could see many beautiful women and handsome guys, dressed up very smartly. This is indeed a strange world.

My wife and I often joke about the fact we'll end up with six or more properties and very old and unsexy underwear full of holes that we'll hang out to dry with old wooden pegs with rusted springs while the drizzle comes down on us and neighbours feel sorry about our difficult life. Given my reticence to spend money on things which I do not deem important, this joke is starting to become a reality.

Jokes apart, many people spend a lot of money on clothing which is just too much for the life they're living: if you're working in finance, law or media, and working in the City you might want to dress accordingly, however, if you're in the middle of nowhere, wouldn't it be better to spend that money for a holiday? Experiences or investing?

In general

Try to think when possible in terms of assets and liabilities, try to focus on your assets, use the things you have as assets to generate value, cut the liabilities if you cannot eliminate them completely, but make them almost irrelevant and then repeat the process.

Spending habits

Now that we have done a general review of your bills, expenses and main assets and liabilities, let's look at another important point: your (our) spending habits. Again, I am not advocating the destruction of the capitalistic system we all rely on to make money and enjoy our lives, however, if you're reading this book **you want to be more of a producer and less of a consumer**, more of a movie director and less of a spectator so let's try to get in the driving seat with our spending also.

Remember, paying off the mortgage, saving, investing, and getting some returns is what we're trying to achieve here, as quickly as possible.

The big one: holidays

For many years, as with every good international professional or economic migrant (basically the same) my family has been asking me: "Are you coming home for Christmas?", "What's your plan for this summer?", "What about Easter?".

Each time this question was asked it was like a £500 punch in the stomach to pay for overpriced air tickets, at peak time, to honour some ancient traditions and give my hard-earned money during the cold, dark and wet British winter to Mr. Ryanair. After doing this for a number of years it became obvious to me that this was just too stupid to continue, and I started to bluntly refuse to engage in this yearly transhumance.

Finally I was free to optimise my holidays, or so I thought, but then my wife started asking to go to the spa she had heard about (and we ended up in a place full of eighty years old) or to go to the all-inclusive hotel (next to a seaside which was not so amazing).

After a number of failed holidays, we decided to change tactics and ended up in Iceland, sleeping in a car and watching the midnight sun or enjoying the Spanish islands. It's not how much you spend; it's *how* you spend.

Let's go back in time, let's go back to the time when we were young and starting to explore the world outside our hometowns. We were travelling by train, bus, sleeping on a beach, talking with random strangers, making friends with the hippies and the gypsies, with the street walker and with the drunkard, with the Irish guitarist and the French busker. Those were interesting times!

Then, all of a sudden, we had some money and we couldn't do those things, take those risks, make those crazy memories and so on. Or can we?

The quality of your holiday and how much money you spend are rarely related, keep this in mind.

You use the money to buy the time and the basics, but money cannot buy the experience. Money is an enabler to amplify what you are and what you dare to be, but you need something to amplify, otherwise you will simply amplify the void.
So go and enjoy your holidays… for real.

Takeaway – your life, bite after bite

In the UK we're particularly guilty of this one: it's been a tiring week, the fridge is empty, the Chinese takeaway makes Gongbao chicken, and I'm shattered. Log in to Just-Eat and spend £35 pounds for a meal for two people, eaten at home in less than fifteen minutes. If my grandmother saw that she would go crazy.

When I was growing up, eating out was a special occasion, eating a pizza or arancini was something we would do on a Saturday night and the four of us would probably spend less than 20 euros. Fast forward fifteen years and we're spending £35 pounds for two people, possibly twice per week.

Last year, after a very tiring period, my wife and I were doing exactly that and it was starting to get out of control: £35 per meal x 2 meals per week x 4 weeks in a month = £280. We all want to get a pizza or a Chinese every now and then, but try to bring that £35 down to £20 and that twice per week to once.

You save money, save yourself, eat healthier food and develop good habits.

The other big one: the house improvements

Yes, that front yard can wait, so can that window and you don't need to repaint everything every year (and in the process inhale loads of toxic VOCs).

Conclusion

For the sake of practicality, I'm stopping here, the message of this section is simple: spend less, spend well. Live a simpler, healthier, lighter, freer, less stressful life, develop good habits and make tons of money to invest in the process. It's a win-win, you just need to go shopping before the fridge gets empty, rediscover the adventurer teenager in you while on holidays and avoid the trap of home improvement, clothing obsession and the "this is how ideally it should be" – too expensive!

Specialisation

Before moving onto the next phase, I want to emphasise the importance of specialisation. If you've found a job where you get better and better every day (remember this is an essential caveat), you'll be getting more and more adept in a very specific field.

It may be the manufacturing of inline skates, of horse food, of genetic sequencing instrumentation, of specialty scissors, couplings, building materials and so on. But it may also be a deep understanding of how the real estate market works, or of how to sell software solutions to the public sector, or of how to perform stylish haircuts on millionaire footballers. You may be on the road to becoming a master gardener, a great journalist, a famous chef or an expert mechanic.

It really doesn't matter.

What matters is that, every day, you're going beyond what you're supposed to do: standard efforts bring standard results, extraordinary efforts bring extraordinary results. This means being active in your work, using your workplace as a way to learn as much as possible, actively seeking opportunities to learn and test new things, new ideas, new skills. Once back home, review those skills, study the market, understand what the competition is, who the competitors are, what the unique selling points are, how things can be done better and faster and so forth.

The past six chapters are likely to cover the next two to five years of your life, from the time you end up in a foreign land or even if you stay in your hometown, to the time you have some sort of stability. **It's not a commitment of a few days or weeks, it's a way of thinking, a way of living, a way of not giving up and persisting until 'The Plan' has been executed.**

And you will face obstacles, doubts, difficulties, it may take longer than expected, you may be living in the middle of a massive economic crash, political or personal instability, and so forth. However, in all this chaos there's great news for you and something you can trust:

Money is neutral

If you do the right things, consistently, money will naturally flow into your bank account.

So keep specialising, keep searching for that edge, for that extra bit of knowledge, for savoir-faire, for enlightenment that will help you earn more, save more, and invest more.

Level 2

*Property portfolio
and
your other business*

Don't wait to buy real estate, buy real estate and wait.
T. Harv Eker

Chapter 7 – Your Own Business

Years ago, while trying to understand the nature of money, business, and how to really make some money, I came across a masterpiece: 'How to Get Rich' by Felix Dennis. Like many other books on the subject, this one is rather philosophical and doesn't give enough guidance to the uninitiated. In that book, however, there's a sentence which is all that you really need to know about money:

> *"The world is full of money.*
> *Some of it has my name on it.*
> *All I have to do is collect it."*

Years after reading the book, I finally comprehended what Felix Dennis meant by this. Below, you can find my attempt to explain this in a few paragraphs, in a practical and accessible way, but you probably won't fully get it until you actually get it by doing business and making money.

The world is full of money

After this Coronavirus crisis, I'm pretty confident that central banks will continue to inject liquidity into the system, to support investment, spending and the recovery of the economy. We're in a globalised market where you can manufacture handmade pottery in France and sell it to China, or manufacture some high-tech device in China and sell it to Mexico.

New people are born every day, millions of people become adults, start families, and buy houses every year. The world is literally booming with people, ideas and opportunities. We might argue that we are too many, that there are ecological impacts, and that the situation is unsustainable. But we might also look at the opportunities for a better world, where resources are better allocated, energy is optimised, food production and delivery are improved, and so on.

Look at yourself and at all the money you've spent on things during the last ten years, directly and indirectly (industrial sector, power, energy), multiply that for seven billion people and you get a vague feeling of how much money exists in the world.

Some of it has my name on it.

Not all of it, not even a small percentage, just some of it has your name on it, and that is much more than enough. Now, up to a certain point you can decide which notes and coins have your name on it, but, at this point in your life, much of it is already determined in one way or another.

If you're thirty years old, it's not very likely that you'll earn the wage of a footballer, you're simply too old to become a footballer now. If you've never studied physics, there will be some money that is not yours, but belongs to the physicists working at CERN in Geneva.

On the other hand, if you're an artist, there's certainly a lot of money that potentially has your name on it in the arts sector, you just need to find it. Likewise if you're a plumber, a lot of money in your local area and beyond will have your name on it – but mind, do not try to get the money that belongs to the financial analyst specialised in portfolio management, nor the money that belongs to the organic farmer, that money probably does not have your name on it.

Follow the money, follow the money that has your name on it. You may dream about getting the money of the footballer or of the corrupt politician and using it for the good of humanity, but that money does not belong to you. You MUST focus on what brings you money, on your own money.

In simple terms:

**TAKE THE MONEY YOU CAN TAKE
DO NOT CHASE THE MONEY YOU WOULD LIKE TO TAKE
TAKE THE MONEY THAT BELONGS TO YOU
DO NOT DREAM ABOUT THE MONEY THAT BELONGS
TO SOMEONE ELSE**

All I have to do is collect it

Once you have identified which is your money, you need to collect it, that is it.

- If you're a barber, you open the shop, organise it, cut hair, collect money.
- If you're a baker, you open the shop, bake good food, collect the money.
- As a web designer, you market yourself, build websites, collect the money.
- If you're a mechanical engineer, you design a machine, get it produced, sell it, and collect the money.

It is really THAT simple... except that it's not! Let's see why, and how, we can move past this theoretical point.

From this point on, I will assume the following:

- You've bought your first house and paid a chunk of the mortgage
- You've got some buffer money in the bank
- You've optimised your expenses
- You are saving a chunk of money every month
- You're growing more and more specialised in your field

The first step
DO NOT open your business

Most people make a huge mistake: they OPEN a business.

Here in the UK (and also more and more in other countries), the act of opening a business is getting easier and easier. To register a limited company, it takes around £100 and 24 hours if you do it through an accountant. So, opening and registering a business isn't really a big deal. It might be a historic moment, a special time for you and your family, you might want to walk to the top of a hill and breathe the fresh moorland air while keeping the incorporation certificate in your hands but sorry, you don't actually have a business, that's not how it works.

Type of businesses

To start trading you don't need a limited company, indeed, at the beginning, you don't need much at all. In the UK[8]:

- You can earn up to £1,000 a year **tax-free** without having to declare this to the taxman. In many countries you can earn up to a certain amount without declaring it and above a certain amount you declare it and pay a tax.
- If you earn more than £1,000 a year, you then must declare this to the taxman in the form of self-assessment. At this point you're probably going to be a **sole trader**.
- Depending on the business, you may decide to start a **partnership**, with another person, to bring someone else into the company, more skills, more knowledge and more capital.
- Finally, you can have a **limited company** (Ltd. in the UK, Llc in the US, Srl in Italy, Gmbh in Germany and so on) which is what many people refer to as a 'real' company.

We will not discuss other forms of companies since they are way beyond the scope of this book. So now you have, my very personal understanding of the four structures you can have in a business:

- Tax free
- Sole Trader/Self-Employed
- Partnership
- Limited Company

---

[8] This is not specialised advice, take everything with a pinch of salt and always consult a specialist

Please note, it is not a progression. Obviously, you can't stay tax free for long, but you could be a sole trader and make substantial amounts of money without having to register a limited company. Also, always talk with a specialised accountant - they know better than me and you.

The main difference between these four models has to do with structure, ownership, and liability. Let's look at the first step.

From Tax Free to Sole Trader

Part 1 (Theory)

James is a handyman and he does odd jobs every now and then. Last winter his neighbour asked him to repair his roof which he did for £300. Two months later Jenny asked him to repair her leaking tap which he did for £50. Another three months go by and Vivienne asks him to rebed her lawn which he does for £650. James has now reached the limit of what he can earn without having to inform the taxman.

Now James has two choices (we won't discuss the third one):

- He can stop doing odd jobs until the clock resets for the financial year (from the 6th April to the 5th April of the following year in the UK)
- He can take on more jobs and then do a self-assessment (a declaration to the taxman)

He decides to keep working and during that financial year he earns £3,500 from his odd jobs. For each job, he issues a simple invoice with his name, address, phone number and bank details. At the same time, James works full time for another company and he is happy to continue like this.

Exercise – Research

Do some research on the following points:
- How you can start your own activity in your own country
- What's the limit for tax-free and how much percentage you'd pay in taxes above that
- How to put together an invoice
- What happens when you make money while you're employed by another company

End of the exercise

At the end of the financial year, on the 5th of April, James sends to his accountant:

- all the invoices he has issued to his customers for his handyman jobs (money in)
- all the invoices for the materials that he has bought to carry out those jobs (money out)

James, is a very methodical person, so once he decided to go beyond the tax-free limit and take more jobs he did a number of things:

- Opened a bank account where all the money related to this activity was going in and out
- Made an Excel spreadsheet to keep track of money in (income) and money out (expenditure)
- Made an invoice template
- Registered an email address for the business activities
- Kept a folder on the Cloud with all the information about each job
- Made sure to keep all his payslips for the last financial year and got a certificate of paid taxes from his employer (P60 in the UK)

A few days later, his accountant had worked her magic and found out that James had made a profit of £1,900 before tax for that year. James will then pay a certain amount of taxes directly to the taxman and he will be done for the year.

Important!

Most people in most countries fear money, taxes, the taxman, accountants, and doing business. In some cases, this is a rational fear since certain systems tend to punish entrepreneurs, but in other cases, the fear is irrational and based on lack of knowledge. What you need to do is talk with an accountant, talk with people in business near you and ask them, what you should do, how to do it, and what to look out for. They are usually very willing to help!

Part 2 (Exercise)

Now you've got the gist of it, I want you to do an exercise.

If you're reading this book, you probably want to make money, be financially independent, possibly leave your job and in the future live from your investments, passive income and your own business. Dreams are good to keep us going!

As said at the beginning of this chapter, I assume you've put in practice most of the things in Part 1 of this book, so you're now a specialised person with a set of specific skills in a certain sector that you can use in that sector and potentially in other sectors too.

Now I need you to MAKE MONEY.

1. **Think of a useful service that YOU can provide or something that you can produce in a sector that you KNOW and UNDERSTAND**
   This could be: fixing computers, giving haircuts, doing nails, web design, assembling pipes, CNC programming, AutoCAD design, helping students with their VISA application, connecting the public and private sectors in a specific field, baking cakes, selling basketball equipment, growing organic food, teaching an instrument, languages or yoga, offering accounting services to small start-ups, and so on.

2. **DECIDE that, for the next twelve months you're going to SERIOUSLY work on this idea**
   You don't need a magic idea that will somehow make you millions of pounds. You need something **you can do**, that people / companies / governments are ready to pay you for, and you need to do it well enough. Most importantly, you need to DECIDE that you will spend a couple of hours every day, after work, working on this and possibly more hours during the weekends and days off.

3. **Make a plan ... that will probably be too optimistic**
   It doesn't have to be detailed. I'll give you an example below.

4. **Implement the plan – basically, work and work hard**
   This is where you make the difference from thinking about having a business to building a business.

At this stage, you don't really want to think about things like: "Which bank should I choose?", "Limited company or sole trader?", "Which one is the best accountant?", "Can my home be my office?".

At this stage, we want to focus on **EVERYTHING that you can do to prepare your business**, while spending little to no money, before you even start looking for customers.

Please, have a go at this exercise and then compare it with the two examples below. There's no right or wrong, unless we actually test the strategy in a specific market at a specific time. Also, please keep in mind that your first attempt will probably fail and you'll have to try a couple of times before you get your business right.

This is all about learning by doing, you need to try and accept the fact that it probably won't work, but you won't have wasted time if you then persist and move onto the next idea, and the next idea, and the next idea after that.

Part 3 - Example exercise 1

1. I've been in the cleaning business for years and I understand the level of cleanliness that customers expect; moreover, with Coronavirus, this is a sensitive issue, and I know how to do deep cleaning because I have attended a number of courses.

2. My usual working hours are from 7:00 to 15:00. My company has a non-competition clause in my contract; however, their market is specific for office cleaning and they do NOT serve families and individuals. This means that, after work, I could do from 16:00 to 19:00 every day and weekend from 11:00 to 16:00. Let's give it a try for three to six months and then see how I get along.

3. My plan is the following:
    a. Register a website for £10 on GoDaddy or any other providers
    b. Work on a simple website with five pages, use an existing template
    c. Work on SEO to be found in the local area
    d. Make the relevant social media pages and all the free marketing
    e. Open a Google Business account for free
    f. Check for legal requirements surrounding this idea
    g. Make an email address, invoice template, forms for the customers, separate phone number and other basic admin
    h. Get a basic cleaning kit to start with
    i. Send an email to all my friends and ask them personally to help me find customers
    j. Print 5,000 leaflets and have them delivered over the weekend
    k. See how it goes and then decide how to proceed

4. The tough part:
    a. Getting the first customer
    b. Working after standard working hours
    c. Juggling and keeping track of everything

If you follow these steps and work very hard at them, you might end up with your own cleaning business within a few months.

Part 3 - Example exercise 2

1. I'm quite good at designing parts in AutoCAD for companies in the industrial sector. Bigger companies have their own designer, however smaller companies might hire freelancers.

2. This doesn't represent a conflict with my full-time job and I really enjoy doing it. I could work on this from 18:00 to 22:00 every day during the week and then eight hours on Saturday and Sunday. Let's go for it and try it for one year to see where it goes.

3. My plan is the following:
    a. Register a website for £10 on GoDaddy or any other provider
    b. Work on a simple website with ten pages, make a nice template, add my portfolio
    c. Make sure the content is well presented and professional
    d. Create a basic presence on the internet (Google, social media etc.)
    e. Make a list of all the businesses that work in the industrial manufacturing sector
    f. Send them personalised introduction emails with an offer of a demo service
    g. Call the important ones during lunch time to discuss potential projects

4. The tough part: do it

Part 3 - Your exercise

Pen and paper and off you go, now!

Part 4 - The thought process

You've probably already noticed, but what I'm describing here is a very simple yet effective thought process. Let's look at it in detail.

Step 1: What is my experience? What do I really know? Why does my current employer pay me? How can I use this skill to provide a service that adds value to someone else? What is the value I can add?

Step 2: What are the resources I have in terms of time and energy to implement this? Do I really want to do it? Can I do it? How long can I try this before giving up?

Step 3: What would be a simple plan? How do I present myself? Website, internet presence? How can I establish credibility? How can I attract customers? Leaflets? Emails? LinkedIn? Cold calling? When can I offer the service? When can I discuss the projects/jobs?

Step 4: Implementation with a simple structure as tax-free sole trader

NOTICE: EVERYTHING TO THIS POINT IS PERFECTLY FEASIBLE

Paperwork, Admin and Practicalities

Before moving on to discuss other matters, it's important to give you some basic guidance on this very boring yet essential part of the business. My focus is mainly on the practical side of things, so it would be unfair to hide from you the boring-but-necessary, which is also what usually scares people at the beginning – before they realise that the really scary bit is when they can't find enough customers.

Basic setup

If you've really decided to go for it, my suggestion would be to open a separate bank account, put £200 in it, make a folder in the Cloud, register an email address, register a website using the money from that bank account and start working on it. From this moment on, all the money from the business goes in and out of that bank account, and you do not touch it – unless your accountant tells you that you can. Website and one year of hosting should not cost more than £30 for the first year at this level.

Intermediate setup

Once your website is decent and contains some basic information (Home, Product/Service, About Us, Contacts, Terms and Conditions, Privacy Policy), make sure you add a phone number, an email address, make sure everything works and that you're registered on Google My Business (they send you a postcard with a code to verify your address). Also, make sure you have a document with your bank details (account number and sort code for national payments, IBAN/SWIFT for international payments) to send to your customers to make bank transfers into your account, a model for an invoice, some basic terms and conditions, and the equipment you need.

Also, you'll probably want to have a folder for your invoices and one for your bills, an Excel spreadsheet where you keep track of your income and expenditure. Also, number your invoices and bills so that your accountant won't hate you at the end of the year.

Advanced setup

Depending on the business, you may want to put a GDPR notice on the website if you use cookies, write more complete terms and conditions, use an accounting system like XERO (very easy to use), and upgrade your bank account.

More paperwork: the importance of accounting

Try to keep things tidy! It's boring and nobody wants to do it, but it has value. All the money that you spend on your business is money that you can detract from your gross profit as an expense, which means that you will be taxed only on your real profit.

For simplicity, let's assume that you're the cleaner and you do NOT keep the invoices for the expenses. This is roughly what happens:

Gross profit for the year: £4,000
Recorded expenses: £0
Net profit (before taxes): £4,000 - £0 = £4,000
20% taxation on the net profit: £4,000 x 0.2 = £800
Net profit after tax: £4,000 - £800 = £3,200[9]

There are two big problems:
1. You have no idea how much money you really made
2. You paid £800 of taxes, which is more than you had to

If you had kept the invoices, however, your numbers would look like:

Gross profit for the Year: £4,000
Registered expenses: £1,000
Net profit (before taxes): £4,000 - £1,000 = £3,000
20% taxation on the net profit: £3,000 x 0.2 = £600
Net profit after tax: £3,200 - £600 = £2,600

In this case you:
1. know how much money you really made (£2,600)
2. saved £200 in taxes

---

[9] We assume here that you are paying 20% income tax

Congratulations! You now have a business!

Dear Reader,

I hope this email finds you well.

Following your previous email, I really do want to offer my congratulations for finally getting to this point.

When, some years ago, we talked about these strategies and *modus operandi*, I was quite sceptical: having been in business for more than a decade, I've seen many people discussing their great ideas, their amazing plans and grand marketing schemes for hours and hours, only for them to discard those very amazing plans a few hours, days and weeks later.

It is the implementation that makes the difference.

It takes a certain character to persist despite the adversities that life throws at us and to continue to pursue one's dream. We do well realise that this is an unequal struggle against history and fate: how can you plan and persist, when the scenario you are operating in keeps changing every few weeks? How can we hope to create something big when it seems that monopolies have taken everything? How can you invest for the long term, when all the threats feel so near?

This is the dilemma of our age.

Yet, reality is so complex and variegated that, as you have seen, if you persist enough, keep trying, keep changing, keep adapting, eventually you will get a share of the wealth that exists in the world, and you will have your own business. You now understand what Felix meant when he said: "Some of it has my name on it".

You're now at a very good point in your life: you've got some sort of financial security, a house, a friendly tenant, you and your wife have both got full-time jobs, and you have this side business that you've been running successfully for some time.

Certainly, you're still a long way away from leaving your full-time job (and why would you anyway since your side business can be run alongside it?) or from making millions, but if you compare that to a few years ago when you had nothing at all, this is already a massive improvement.

However, I've been in business long enough and I know that the real challenge starts now: growing your business, as well as your wealth. I am confident that, since you got so far, you will not give up now.

Best of luck and kind regards,   Mr. Bill SilverStone

Chapter 8 – 發, Growing Wealth

In this vision of wealth generation and accumulation, there isn't a simple formula where you implement one thing, the whole time, and get a certain result. It's a complex structure where personal development, saving, investing, entrepreneurship, real estate, selling and innovation all play a role.

This is the formula I think can work, on average, for people in their twenties and thirties in the decade starting in 2020s in the West and the developed world.

We're not in an era of booming property markets, so you cannot simply try to become the millionaire real estate investor in France, the US or Italy. However, property prices are rising, the population is increasing, and rents are increasing too. Not booming, but still increasing in certain areas.

We're also not in an era where companies are getting access to vast new markets to export to or where vast swathes of the population are seeing their wages increase massively (at least in the West). On the contrary, wages are stagnating in most of Europe/US or growing very slowly. Not booming, but marginally improving.

Finally, we're not (yet) in the next great revolution, it seems we're more like in a transition towards AI, quantum computers, CRISPR editing and genomic medicine, we can see and imagine them, but while they are starting to shape the new world it's still too early for them to really revolutionise the world. Not there but getting there - strategic positioning is very important in this respect.

So, in this context, what I think makes sense is playing a game with three or four points:

- Personal development of contacts, skills and knowledge in specific fields (and potentially some strategic positioning for the world that will come)
- Moderate investment into real estate
- Investment of time and effort into building a sustainable business
- Other financial investments

In this strategy, the real estate portfolio has several functions:

- Intercept the long-term growth
- Be a wealth buffer for the old age and the next generation
- Provide some cash flow support in the medium-long term
- Provide access to job markets in different locations

The personal development is useful for:

- You own company
- Yourself
- Your position in the job market

Your own company is useful for:

- Giving you a chance to intercept exponential/accelerated growth
- Keep you busy and not bored
- Providing an extra income
- Flexibility and freedom to work from different locations

Other investments are useful for:

- Differentiation
- Learning
- Contacts

Now we have clarified the logic behind these choices, let's look at what we did and what you could learn from it.

A real story of money and life

In order to keep some level of credibility, I'll share some details with you about what my wife and I have done and how we have ended up with three houses and three mortgages that pay for themselves and are starting to produce an income (seven years after the first purchase), a business that is working well and a healthy bank balance.

<u>There is always a past</u>

Before following me to the UK, my wife was working while living with her parents for a few years. During those years she saved a lot of money. My wife and I are quite similar in the sense that we focus on the substance rather than on appearances, which means that we never spent money on status symbol goods and rarely on irrelevant things.

<u>Baby steps</u>

By the time she joined me in the UK, she had already saved a good amount of money and, in 2013, combining some of my savings, some of her savings and some money that my parents gave me we bought our first house outright for the incredible price of £45,000 in a small town in the north of England where nobody wanted to live.

In a way, us putting money together to work towards a common goal was probably the point where we committed to each other fully. The wedding, celebrated cheaply years later, was more of a formality of something that had been decided many years earlier.

There are a few events and choices which are important to notice:

- In 2011, aged 26 and after twenty days in London, I decided to leave London because it wasn't possible for me to 'make a life' there (basically buy a house and have a normal life); that decision was taken within three weeks of me being in the city.
- When I was looking for a job, I targeted areas where it was cheaper to live and to make a life but still with some good-sized cities, namely the north of England.
- Between 2011 and 2013, I tried to save as much as I could and to improve my skills as much as possible. I ended up staying in the same company for four years (for two years I was renting, for two years I was a mortgage-free homeowner) to create a stronger financial situation.
- My parents gave me some money (around £15,000) which was used to pay for the house outright and for some substantial improvement works.
- The house we bought wasn't amazing, needed a lot of work done and for the first few weeks we were sleeping on the floor, with workers going in and out trying to make the bathroom and kitchen usable, and assembling IKEA furniture bit by bit – we did NOT want to pay an extra month or two of rent to have a 'smooth' transition, we really wanted to save that £800!
- Between 2011 and 2013, my wife didn't work and focused on learning English and overcoming some social anxiety issues, which meant that my £1,300 a month really had to last.
- We didn't go on any special holidays; most of our time was spent working, studying and trying to keep fit.
- During those four years we always rented out the second room to various people (guys and girls) to help to pay for the bills and the car that was bought AFTER the house.

I could've told you that, through hard work and saving a lot of money, we were able to get our first mortgage, that nobody helped us, that we made it ourselves, but it wouldn't be fair and the numbers would not add up. At the same time, when I was in the middle of that process, nobody explained to me all the things I'm telling you in this book, I had to make mistakes and find my own way, which meant that time was lost trying to find the formulas I'm now sharing with you.

Obviously, being able to buy outright, without having to take out a mortgage, was a huge help for a migrant in a foreign land, with no relatives in sight and very few friends. You might not have that money coming from your parents or your spouse, but you might have some advantages compared with me and my wife at the time. The message is: each story is different but the principles are the same.

Had I decided to stay in London, or to buy a £200,000 house, or to take on a big mortgage or to live in a 'posh' area, it would've been impossible for me and my wife to end up with three properties, a business and all the other financial certainties that we have now.

Houses and Bananas!

In 2015, we went bananas: left our jobs, went on holidays to Thailand, opened a web design company (a limited company) without the knowledge and then ended up looking for a job again within a few months since our bank account was plummeting. It was at that point that I started to realise the power of property investment and of renting properties.

Having found a new job and living with my wife literally under the roof of a shared property – a small room created in an attic space by a nice landlady – we decided to rent out the first house because "we didn't like it to be empty". We spent a couple of weeks moving all our stuff out and decorating at the weekends. My wife went and stayed over a number of days, fighting with wallpaper, glue and the vacuum cleaner.

Once ready, we put out an advert through a website called OpenRent at a very reasonable price and, within a few days, the house was rented out to a guy who had broken up with his ex-partner after she tried to hurt him badly. We were happy, he was happy, everybody was happy.

Less than six months into my new job, I realised that the company I had joined, while paying much more than my previous employer, was a basket case of nepotism, extravagance and constructive dismissals. At the same time (winter 2016) Brexit was approaching and being a little more well-versed in money, business and human nature, I decided that we NEEDED to buy a new house and stop renting and living with two other people.

There were several motivations for this step:

1. I had fully grasped the gravity of paying rent and did not want to do it, unless strictly necessary
2. We needed space: all our stuff was out of the house and cramped in an attic and a small room
3. My current employer was crazy and I needed some stability
4. We wanted a better cash flow

5. Last but not least, we wanted to get some positive outcome from Brexit – cynicism always helps.

So we started to look for our second house.

The second house

Given the uncertainty created by Brexit, the mood swings of my current employer, the fact that my wife was commuting by public transport one hour each way to her new workplace and I was commuting thirty-five minutes by car in the opposite direction, I had a very difficult task in finding a house.

We started to look around for opportunities but prices in the local area were quite high and, given the general situation, we didn't want to take on too much risk. After weeks spent looking at different properties, prices, commuting distances, train connections, mortgage repayment forecasts and so on, we found what we needed.

These were the criteria we followed:

- It had to be in a safe area
- It shouldn't cost a lot (£80,000 maximum) because we didn't want to empty our bank account
- It should have a second bedroom to rent out as soon as we moved in
- It should be located in such a way that at least my wife could be next to her job and avoid driving more than fifteen minutes
- It should allow me to get to work in maximum two hours (door to door) by public transport

And so we got our first mortgage approved and, two weeks after Brexit, bought a property that was on the market for £85,000, at the Brexit price of £72,000. As Europeans in Brexit Britain we did exactly this:

***Buy when there's blood in the streets,
even if the blood is your own***

In August 2016, we got the key to our second house and we restarted the process of upgrading the house, assembling furniture, optimising bills, moving accounts and so forth. The joys of paperwork and of moving home…

The commuter

The following twelve months were very tiring since, at the same time, I was:

- Commuting four hours per day by changing two trains
- Studying at the Open University to improve my understanding of chemistry

- Dealing with constructive dismissal which was clearly underway for my whole department
- Applying for my British citizenship within the hostile environment fostered by Theresa May's government
- Trying to understand how to make money... obviously!

Some lessons were learnt during that year:

- Commuting longer than one hour should never be a permanent solution
- You can get a degree while commuting on the train
- When you see that your department is going under, it's important to change your job before your company decides to "change you"
- In a dysfunctional company, there are huge spaces for you to focus on your own activities: use it!
- Everybody has a plan that won't work

After almost twelve months, emotionally and physically drained, I was told by my line manager that my position was being made redundant. Luckily, by that time, I already had two job offers, so I smiled and told them: "That's fine, I have another two jobs lined up. Oh and by the way, remember that:

The snake which cannot cast its skin has to die. As well the minds which are prevented from changing their opinions; they cease to be minds."[10]

Years later, that dysfunctional company, unable to evolve and change its mind on how to treat business partners with respect, is facing increasing losses with the managers trapped in it. My company instead is growing together with my wealth. If you have to be a snake, you must cast your skin every now and then.

<u>Choices</u>

At this point I was faced with an interesting choice:

Job Offer 1:	Job Offer 2:
<ul><li>New sector and a cool team</li><li>Fifteen minutes from my second home</li><li>£45,000 per year</li><li>Established company</li></ul>	<ul><li>Same sector where I had worked for four years</li><li>New city, commuting not possible</li><li>£38,000 per year</li><li>Smaller company</li></ul>

---

[10] A famous quote of Friedrich Wilhelm Nietzsche

Which one did I choose? The second one.

At first, this choice could seem completely irrational: why would you, within one year of buying your second home, decide to move to a new city (a 'beta' global city), for less money, in a clearly unstable company and go through all the renting-buying process again? It did not make much sense, except that it did to make money.

By that time I had realised that, having spent four successful years in a company within a specific sector and then two more years in a somehow related sector, if I wanted to open my own business I needed to use my connections, knowledge and network and, to do so, I needed my new job to be in the same sector of my own business.

Also, by that time, my eyes were focused to establish myself and my wife in a bigger city, with more opportunities, near a major airport and to differentiate the geographical spread of my little property empire. And the only way to do that was to get a pay cut, make a bet for this innovative start-up and to hope that the bet paid off.

New job, new city, the third house and the business

I moved again (this time alone) into a rented room for around four months while my wife continued working at her usual job and focused all my energy to establish a customer base in the new company. Later, I started to rent an apartment and moved most of our stuff from the second house to the new rented apartment. All this while my wife still kept living in the other city and working at the same place so that she had the stable job history required to apply for a mortgage.

At the same time, we were already looking at properties in the area and filing a lot of paperwork to get an equity release from my first house[11]. In fact, that house that we originally bought for £45,000, through sweat value and improvements, was now worth £65,000 and by releasing equity we were able to raise £40,000 for the deposit for the third house.

A few days before my one year anniversary in my new job, I was stepping into my third house, in a beta global city in England, with two bedrooms, two living rooms, a kitchen, a storage unit (just in case we decided to rent everything and run away) and a basement that could be used as an office for my company. After twelve months in our new home, we registered our own business and that changed the game altogether.

---

[11] You can release equity (money) from a house you own. If you buy the house for £100,000 and then it grows in value to £130,000 and you have already paid £20,000, you might be able to release that money and use that money to buy another house.

Compromises, hard work, patience, endurance, and laser focus

We'll look at some of the aspects in more detail in the following pages and chapters, however, it's important to understand why this approach has worked and **the price we had to pay**.

1. The focus has always been on establishing security and stability in a world gone bananas. Yes, we wanted to go out partying those Saturday evenings but we also wanted a feeling of security.
2. For long periods we have been very flexible: working and living far from each other, my wife was getting any job possible to keep the money rolling in, I was commuting four hours per day to make the investment work, she was redecorating the house and putting up with numerous house moves.
3. We worked hard, we really worked hard at our jobs to keep them, improve and make it work.
4. Comfort was not a priority…at all.
5. Paperwork, paperwork, paperwork, paperwork, paperwork.

A timeline

Before concluding this section, I want to share a timeline with you.

I started this journey when I was twenty-six, we have been through the 2008 financial crisis, the 2010-2013 recession that has affected my home country and job prospects there, the Brexit saga, and now Coronavirus. So, if you're starting out now and you're in your twenties and you think: "well, you had it easy", think again. Having said that, this is not a scheme to get rich quick, since I have no idea on how to do that, however, it is a scheme that has increased our net worth from around £20,000 to almost £300,000 in seven years, and it's growing faster and faster.

A timeline for your benefit:

2008 - 2011
- Completing my degree, working briefly in Hong Kong
- Meeting my wife, while she was working and saving money

February - March 2011
- Arrived in London with a laptop, a degree and 2,000 euros
- Looked for and found a job
- Started working in a specialised job

From March 2011 to August 2013
- Saved money and studied my job to become more qualified
- Improved language and scientific skills, studied sales and selling techniques
- Supported my wife to learn English and become acclimatised to the UK

- Made friends with a local estate agent who helped us…

September 2013
- ….to buy our first house for £45,000, where the kitchen and bathroom were a disaster
- And that was paid in full

October 2013 – March 2015
- Continued to save money and live a simple life and got caught in the rat race
- My wife started to work and started to study web design and then… we went bananas!

April 2015 – August 2015
- Trip to Thailand and Singapore
- Opened a limited company to sell web design - I was cold calling ten hours per day, my wife working on projects twelve hours per day; we put some stickers on the car saying "We do web design"
- Financial despair and…

The Slough of Despond

That very summer, while walking in the Forest of Bowland on a hill, I actually ended up in a deep bog. It was an enlightening moment because I was quite high up on the hill and still, such a deep bog existed. After that, I realised that it was not only my body that was sinking on those sunny uplands in July, but also my bank account, and we needed to change course and quickly.

The Slough of Despond is a fictional, deep bog in John Bunyan's allegory The Pilgrim's Progress, into which the protagonist Christian sinks under the weight of his sins and his sense of guilt for them. (Credit: Sylvester, Charles H. Journeys through Bookland, Volume 5 (Chicago, IL: Bellows-Reeve Company, 1909)

September 2015
- My wife gets a factory job to pay the bills

October 2015
- I get a new job and my wife follows me to a new city
- We rent a room in a house with two other friendly people, thirty minutes' drive from my workplace which was in a very expensive city

November - December 2015
- My wife works on decorating our first house to rent it out

January 2016 - July 2016
- Rent out the first house to the first tenant and learn all the practicalities
- Buy the second house (£72,000) after getting a mortgage with a mortgage broker

August 2016 - August 2017
- Commuting four hours per day while studying at the Open University
- Saving money, looking for a new job, finding a new job

September 2017 - August 2018
- Working at my new job in the new city while renting a room first and then an apartment
- My wife was working at her old job to get the mortgage approved
- Releasing equity from the first house to fund the third house
- Studying the local market in-depth to be ready for the right opportunity
- Buy the third house (£188,000 with a £159,000 mortgage)

August 2018 - Present
- Bring the mortgage down to £133,000 in less than two years
- Launch the company and close many national and international sales
- Added various product lines
- Created a healthy bank account
- Re-organised and re-rationalised the three mortgages

In simple words, a real bloody mess!

The reality of paperwork

When you read (or write) a book on money, business and properties, it's easy to overlook a very important thing: paperwork. Paperwork is the stuff of nightmares, paperwork is never ending and everywhere. Banks, customers, financial institutions, companies, governments, they will all ask for a lot of it, so it's important that you know it exists. Here are some ideas on how to deal with paperwork.

If you move abroad and even if you don't

Whenever you decide to move abroad to start a new life, you must be aware of the importance of paperwork. From your plane ticket with a landing date, to your registration for National Insurance, from your first bank account to the water bills, **you want to keep everything**.

Remember that the world has gone bananas and governments might ask you to prove that you have lived in a country and want documentation for that. Have it with you at all times. You might lose your clothes, your shoes, your laptop, but you should never lose your passport and your paperwork.

What has real value in this world is not the laptop you have in your room, the expensive dress, the big TV or even the car, but it is **the web of established civil ownership and property rights associated with your person**. For this reason, your passport, a traceable work history, property deeds, insurances, mortgages and paperwork in general are extremely important.

As egregiously expressed in the sonata below[12] from *The Beggar's Opera*, whatever you do, it has to be in compliance with the law, to avoid losing it all!

> *A fox may steal your hens, Sir,*
> *A Whore your health and Pence, Sir,*
> *Your daughter rob your Chest, Sir,*
> *Your Wife may steal your Rest, Sir,*
> *A Thief your Goods and Plate,*
> *A Thief your Goods and Plate.*
> *But this is all but picking,*
> *With Rest, Pence, Chest, and Chicken,*
> *It ever was decreed, Sir,*
> *If Lawyer's Hand is fee'd, Sir.*
> *He steals your whole Estate,*
> *He steals your whole Estate*

Mortgages

Since part of our wealth growth strategy is represented by properties and since it's unlikely that you have £500,000 at your disposal, it's highly probable that you'll end up setting up many mortgages. When you apply for a mortgage, you'll need a flurry of paperwork including payslips for the last six months, employment contracts, passports, bank statements, and so on.
Now, to give you an example, since starting this journey my wife and I have applied for many mortgages.

---

[12] 'A Fox May Steal Your Hens, Sir', *The Beggar's Opera*

- Property 1:
    - Equity release mortgage: 2 years fixed, 35 years
    - Renegotiated mortgage for better rate and shorter term: 5 years fixed, 15 years

- Property 2:
    - Original mortgage: 2 years fixed, 35 years
    - Renegotiated mortgage for better rate and shorter term: 5 years fixed, 20 years

- Property 3:
    - Original mortgage: 3 years fixed, 35 years
    - Renegotiated for: 2 years fixed, 15 years term

This involved a lot of paperwork, also because not every application goes smoothly and not every house purchase goes well (we had two house purchases that did not go through).

Self-assessment

Also, as soon as you go from working for a company to having a side job which brings some money and/or having a rental property that generates an income, a new world of paperwork will also emerge.

As we saw a few chapters back, there's only so much you can earn before you need to inform the taxman. This means that, if you're serious about growing wealth, the accountant will become your friend and your judge (they will know you better than yourself!) and you'll also have to file a self-assessment, or tax declaration every year and, if there's two of you, then most likely both you and your partner will have to do it.

Usually, this is just a matter of organisation: open a separate bank account, keep all the receipts, make sure you issue invoices, make sure you keep the invoices, and so on. It helps to keep a folder on the Cloud.

Dealing with paperwork

My strong advice is this: when a new activity starts (a house, a property, a business, a side business, an investment), make sure that you have a physical folder where you organise everything, and also a folder in the Cloud.

Also, don't wait for things to go out of control. Every few weeks, when it's raining, you can't do anything exciting and you want to stay inside, then go through your files and sort them out. Throw away superfluous paper (i.e. mortgage terms and conditions that you can find online), but keep and sort all the essential things, you really want to keep on top of that pile of paperwork, and specifically anything with names, dates and addresses.

Your first Buy-to-Let: Decision and Analysis

As you can probably see from the previous pages, my path was not straightforward since I moved with the jobs, bought houses and then later renegotiated the mortgages into buy-to-let mortgages. You can still rent out your main home on a residential mortgage if you're desperate, but my advice would always be to ask for a 'consent to let', where you ask the bank for the permission to rent your main home and that is usually granted.

Also, your path to wealth will be different, so what I will describe here is a scenario, an idea, a guideline, based on the story of Xiaohui and Jenny.

Two years after having bought their first house (in the fifth year since they started working on this), Xiaohui and Jenny were both promoted and received pay rises and now have around £40,000 in their bank account. They now have some choices when it comes to properties:

- Renegotiate their existing mortgage which is coming to the end of the fixed term (they went for two years fixed) and use part of that £40,000 to lower their mortgage and get a better interest rate.
- Invest in a second property in the form of a buy-to-let (in the UK you need at least a 25% deposit)
- Buy a new house for themselves and convert their existing house into a buy-to-let
- Try a mix of various options

As we now well know, Xiaohui and Jenny are quite good at saving money and, through hard work and dedication, they managed to get good jobs. Xiaohui also started a side-business which for now is not bringing in any substantial income (£500 a month) but is showing signs of growth. Finally, Xiaohui and Jenny are also renting out a room in their own home, so their balance sheet looks something like this (without counting the business):

Money in (£)		Money out (£)	
Xiaohui wage	2,000	Mortgage	450
Jenny wage	2,150	Savings – paid into the account	620
Tenant	300	Gas/electricity	100
		Council tax	120
		Internet	30
		Phone Xiaohui	12
		Phone Jenny	12

		Car finance	230
		Car insurance	60
		Petrol	100
		Food	250
		Eating out	200
		Emergencies	200
		Various miscellanea	100
Total in	4,450	**Total out**	2,484

Which gives them a monthly saving of around £2,000. Let's think about this for a second.

If you remember, we looked at the example of one person who, alone and with no specialisation, was working hard and saving money. This gave him savings of around £3,000 per **year**. Now, a few years later, through some clever choices, Xiaohui and Jenny are saving more than £2,000 a **month**. This point again emphasises the importance of having a long-term plan, investing, making the right choices and creating a web of skills, property rights and income streams.

Even if they were to be stuck in this position, Xiaohui and Jenny, would save £24,000 per year, £240,000 over ten years. If instead someone is stuck saving £3,000 per year with no improvement, plan or investment, after ten years he or she can expect to have a meagre £30,000. I hope you can see the difference and how this difference is created.

Xiaohui and Jenny have also been investing in their home and fixing things, they're quite confident that, in the worst-case scenario (both losing their jobs at the same time), they could survive with less than £1,000 per month. This means that, for each month where everything keeps ticking along, they earn an extra two months of buffer money.

Aware of their numbers and of the recovery speed of their bank balance, they decide that they are comfortable to bring their savings down to £5,000 and use £35,000 for investment. So, the question that they now have is the following: "what should we do?". Below you can see their thought process.

Option 1: Renegotiate their existing mortgage which is coming to an end of the fixed term (they went for two years fixed) and use part of that £35,000 to lower their mortgage and get a better interest rate.

This is the safest possible option and allows you to be mortgage-free very quickly. While it's a good option and you're saving on interest (potentially saving a lot) it also has a limitation: it costs time. If you use that money to pay off the mortgage, it will take you one to two years to save up a new deposit to invest in a property, so it's a safe bet but not the one that works best if you want to grow your wealth.

Option 2: Invest in a second property in the form of a buy-to-let.

This seems like a good option too. With £35,000 to invest, you can use around £28,000 for the deposit, £1,500 for legal fees and transactions, £2,000-£3,000 for taxes and small improvements. With this kind of deposit, you can get a property up to £112,000 which usually buys you a small-medium size house in a decent area.

Getting a mortgage in your name does not mean that you will physically repay that mortgage. It means that you **give a guarantee to the bank that, in any case, they will get paid back the money plus their interest**. This is an important difference.
What you're giving to the bank is your fiscal credibility, your reputation (credit score); what you're not giving them is your money, since it is someone else who will help you to pay for that.

Option 3: Buy a new house for themselves and convert their existing house into a buy-to-let.

This option can also be interesting. Imagine that Xiaohui and Jenny want to move to a bigger and better house. It could make sense to use the deposit to buy a new and bigger house, with a larger deposit and a better interest rate on a bigger sum RATHER THAN buying another investment property and then having to wait some more years or having a smaller deposit on a third house.
Having said that, it's important not to get carried away: if you want to pick the fruits too early, you might end up stuck for a long time in a mediocre growth curve, which is still good but not as good as it could be: the more you reinvest, the quicker you can grow.

Option 4: Try a mix of various options

I'm sorry Jenny, you simply don't have enough money to buy an investment property AND lower your mortgage at the same time. Be realistic.
After careful consideration, Xiaohui and Jenny decided to go for Option 2 and buy their first buy-to-let property.

**THEY WANTED THEIR MONEY TO
WORK HARD FOR THEM
PAST A CERTAIN POINT IT MUST BE THE MONEY
THAT WORKS FOR YOU AND NOT THE OTHER WAY AROUND**

Now they needed to decide the specifications and the location of the property. Let's start from this last point which, I believe, can be strategically important.

Location

The great thing about buying a house is that it's an investment you can live in. If you buy a piece of forest, you might want to camp there but you certainly cannot live there; if you invest in a restaurant, you can't legally sleep in the kitchen; if you invest in the stock market you can't sleep in Wall Street, and so on. With a house, however, it's different, you can live in it.

Let's say that you live in Hanau, near Frankfurt, where you work, and you've bought your first property there. With a house in Hanau, you get access to the job market of Frankfurt, a place you really like.

However, you used to go to the university in Dusseldorf, over two hours away from where you live and, one day, you would like to move to the area because there are more opportunities for you and your family there.

What do you do?

- You buy another house in Frankfurt since you know the area well and have an established net of estate agents and friends who can help you find a good deal
- You buy in Dusseldorf, where you have to start from zero and you know no-one BUT, by working hard and studying the market, you can gain access to a new area

My preferred option has always been the second one since, personally speaking, a house is almost like a base in a strategy game where you're trying to get better and better access to resources and areas where you can score a lot of points. This also allows you to expand the possibilities of your life and makes you more resilient if times get tough.

You can have one big house in a main city, or you can have two small houses and a medium size one in commuter towns near to big cities; the second option gives you access to different cities, natural areas and a more relaxed lifestyle. I know which option I prefer, but it's not a must.

On the other hand, there's also a very strong case for specialisation: it takes months of study to really get a feeling for the housing market in an area, get to know the estate agents and so on.

Also, if you want to manage the house yourself and it's always a two hour drive each way every time the tenant has a problem, it can be an issue, so you need to choose carefully.

Specifications

The house should be in a decent area where it can be easily rented out at a price that should cover at least 125% of the mortgage but it's better if that's around 150-200% of a mortgage for the first period when you're still learning. For this reason, I suggest starting with a long mortgage for thirty-five years and two years fixed, and then renegotiate it once the term is over and, obviously, make all the overpayments you can.

Once you've found houses that fill these criteria then I think it's mainly a matter of personal preferences and of the condition of the house. What you want to look for are:
- Things that can go wrong big time (subsidence, flooding, fires, roofs)
- Things that can cost money (electrical installations, gas, heating system)

What you do NOT need to worry about is how it looks since repainting is a relatively cheap job.

On this my suggestion is to read specialised websites which will give you some good suggestions on prices, things to look out for, and so on.

Exercise – Research your first rental property

- Look for different areas
- Search which areas have the best rental yields
- See how much deposit you need to buy a second house
- Research how much taxes you would pay in your country on a second home
- Get an idea of how much it would cost to do certain repairs
- Run a simulation in Excel or using pen and paper
- Check rental prices

Your first Buy-to-Let: Purchase and Renting

Now that you've decided what to buy and where, the process is relatively easy.

Purchase

What you do is the following:

1. Search for a good mortgage broker who will help you find the best deal
2. Provide them with all the financial information, paperwork etc.
3. They will come back after a few days with a Decision in Principle and then a Mortgage Offer from the bank that will confirm how much they are willing to lend you

4. Meanwhile, you're looking at properties online always keeping in mind those criteria/specifications that you have written down
5. At the same time, you're talking with estate agents in that area and letting them know that you're planning to invest but only for the right opportunity (15-20% below market value)
6. You then **WAIT for the right opportunity**[13], which is usually the property which is easy to rent out, in a decent location and at a price which is low for the local market (perhaps the seller just wants some cash quickly and you can help them out!)
7. You may want to make offers which are 15-20% less than the price you think that house is worth on a number of different houses and see who agrees to sell at a price which is good for you. There isn't the 'right house' but rather the 'right price for the right house'
8. Then once the offer is accepted at the price you like, you push to make everything happen as quickly as possible (calls, emails, visits – keep on top of it)
9. Use this time to get quotes from different builders to get a few necessary repairs done on the house and everything in order. I repeat: get different quotes!
10. You get the keys, **you live in the house for a few days to make sure you know it**, decide if you want to put in furniture or not (depending on the tenants you are targeting) and, as soon as everything is ready and you have your gas and electricity certificates, you put it on the rental market at a REASONABLE price

<u>Renting</u>

Before renting out you really want to be sure that everything works well in the house (boiler, water, gas, taps) and this is the reason why I suggest living in the house for a few days to get a taste of it. You might want to use a week or two of your holidays for this process (**this is the price you pay**) but at least you'll be sure that the house is in very good condition.

When you become a landlord, however, you also start to have **some responsibilities**. Here I'm not talking simply about legal compliance or health and safety regulations, but about people. When someone comes and lives in the home you are renting, you want to give them a place that they will like, where they will feel free and relaxed and where they will have a good life.

Also, while it's important to charge the right amount, **I really disagree with the**

---

[13] That house is not the beautiful house that has been on the market for four months but it's the house that the estate agent is going to put on the market in a few days but gives you some information before that even happens!

idea of charging the maximum possible amount. If you overcharge your tenants, because the market conditions allow you to do so, they will know it and they will feel it. When I was charged £700 per month to rent an apartment south of Manchester (my mortgage, in the same area, for a house three times bigger was £484) I was really resentful towards the agency and had no flexibility at all when it came to standards, regulations and compliance. Also, charging too much means that your tenants will eventually flee the place and you might lose a few weeks or months of rent.

What you really want is to give someone a place to stay at a reasonable price and for as long as possible. They will be grateful and might even help you to find the next tenant when they move out, and you won't have to deal with unreasonable and grumpy people: win-win situation.

On the other hand, the selection of the tenants is particularly important: trust your gut feeling. Do all the checks: check their references personally, look for things that do not match up and, in general, ask yourself the question: "This is my house and I could live there one day: am I comfortable with renting it out to these people?". If the answer is YES, then you have good tenants.

Also, keep in touch with people and try to understand when their situation changes or is going to change. The last thing you want is to invest in a fourth property when the rental income from your first one is going to dry up temporarily.

Finally, remember that you're not a social housing association but, at the same time, if tenants that have always been paying struggle for a few months, do you really want to evict them and create useless stress? As long as they're genuinely trying to improve their situation and working hard towards it, I believe you should give them time if you're in a position to do so.

Agencies

Some people like to rely on agencies since they take care of everything (collecting rent, fixing things), however, many agencies are like vultures and, for as long as possible, I suggest trying to manage everything yourself and keeping a good relationship with the tenants.

Contracts, rent collection, legal compliance

In the UK there's a good website called OpenRent that offers many useful tools for you to manage the tenancies, sign contracts, collect rent and keep on top of everything.

If in your country such a website does not exist, just make a list and a calendar of what you need to do and when, so that you always follow the law.

Final thoughts

As you start making strides in the world of wealth and money there will be two things you will need to pay attention to:
1. You do not want to take advantage of people in a weaker position
2. You do not want to be taken advantage of by people who think they are smarter than you

This is extremely important, and it is a **fine balance** and a difficult line to walk on.
As you meet more people, more businesses, more customers, more tenants, more business partners, you will see all the shades of human nature. As an investor and a businessperson, while remaining human and empathetic, you will have to learn to say "NO" and "that's enough" and make tough decisions when needed. At the same time, whenever possible, you want to help people when/if they are struggling.
This is a skill that you will learn with time.

NOTICE: EVERYTHING TO THIS POINT IS PERFECTLY FEASIBLE

Having rushed through the first two parts of this book (Level 1 and Level 2), I have deliberately left out many topics from the flow of the storytelling. This book aims to be the missing link between being broke/unemployed and being a self-sustaining businessperson/investor. For this reason, I wanted to get your attention by showing you how the numbers work, how the time goes and how to actually make money.

However, It would be disingenuous to think that simply by reading those pages and applying those principles you can make it. There's much more to it and **90% will come from you**, not from me, not from this book, not from any online tutorial, audiobook and so on. You have to do your own research, you will have to specialise in your field, you will have to keep motivated, you will have to bounce back, you must save money, you must refrain from senseless spending, you will have to take commitments in your life, with people, with businesses, with countries and with decisions.

Again, this book is not about becoming a millionaire in three simple steps; it's not some kind of self-brainwashing codswallop about how attitude is everything; I recognise that some of the things I am proposing here are difficult or even impossible in certain contexts (how can I start a business if taxation is so high?) but I also recognise that, being an average person, with a certain level of determination, you can get to the point where you are in the real game of making money (Level 3) but you need to get there, and that takes work, time and discipline.

In the following pages, before getting into Level 3, let's look at some topics in more detail, from a theoretical and from a practical point of view.

I will try to alternate topics so that things don't focus too much on personal development, building a real estate portfolio or growing your own business. I'd like to try and push each of these three things every time, because they're all part of the strategy.

Interphase (the theory)

*Mental patterns,
thoughts and
ideas*

The only limit to our realization of tomorrow will be our doubts of today.
Franklin D. Roosevelt

MOTIVATION

This is the main one: without motivation you can't do much – Mr. Stephen Covey nails this down very well in his book. Making money is the process that you implement to get the money you will use to do or buy something else.

**Price is what you pay, value is what you buy and
money is what you need to buy that value**

Now, if your motivation to make money is because you dream of buying an expensive sports car to impress girls at the local bar, this motivation will fade away as soon as you're in a stable relationship (or at least it should). If your motivation to make money is because you don't want to feel poor, then it will fade away as soon as you have reached a certain level of financial security (Level 1 or 2).

If you want to make money to be able to travel around the world, you really do not need to: by doing odd jobs or working in international trade, you can get to visit most of the world and it's more fun than being in five-star hotels. If you want to make money as a matter of personal pride against this person or that person that belittled you, again, this motivation will fade away as soon as you reach a certain level.

You have to look within yourself and decide what matters to you, what you really want to make of your life, what you believe in, what you want to achieve and how you want to live. That's the reason why Mr. Covey says to "start with the end in mind". Imagine you're watching your funeral, who do you want to be there? What things do you want to be remembered for? How do you want to have lived your life? Or even….do you want a funeral and people to remember you or you want to die fighting gorillas in the jungle?

You need to:
- Think long and hard about what you want to do with your life
- Decide if making money is important to reach your objectives
- Decide the price you are willing to pay in terms of 'unlived life' to get that money
- Follow a relatively safe and proven path
- Collect the money that has your name on it
- Do what you were intending to do all along

Be aware, however, that money earned in this way **might have a stale smell of unlived life**, so pay attention to what you wish for.
In my personal case, for example, money is:
- a way to measure my contribution to human progress
- a past-time to keep busy

- something that enables me to have the fiscal tranquillity to do other things I like such as reading, writing and eventually be involved in politics
- something that allows me to create systems which are more human and sustainable

I won't spend more pages on this. This is not a book about philosophy, the meaning of life, religion, atheism, humanism, Christianity, Buddhism, how to change the world etc. I leave the joy of exploring what you want to do with your limited time here in the world to yourself.

Below the translation of an Italian song about the meaning of life, inspired by some thoughts of Marcus Aurelius, an emperor of the Roman Empire. The song, by Giorgio Gaber, is titled 'Ragiona amico mio'.

Ponder, My Friend	**Ragiona, amico mio**
Ponder, my friend, it might seem strange to you, but at the time of the empire of the great Vespasian you can find those things that, inevitably, also happen now, inexorably. Ponder, my friend, reflect on it for a moment, and try honestly to learn a lesson from it.	Ragiona amico mio potrà sembrarti strano Ma ai tempi dell'impero del grande Vespasiano Ritrovi quelle cose che inevitabilmente Accadono anche adesso inesorabilmente. Ragiona amico mio riflettici un momento E cerca onestamente di trarne insegnamento
You can find many people who love one another and who get married, who give birth to children, who take care of their home. You can find people who get sick, you can find people who make merry, you can find the rich, the peasant, the dishonest people. Ponder, my friend, reflect on it for a moment, and try honestly to learn a lesson from it.	Ritrovi tanta gente che si ama e che si sposa Che mette al mondo figli che cura la sua casa Ritrovi chi si ammala ritrovi chi fa festa Il ricco il contadino la gente disonesta Ragiona amico mio riflettici un momento E cerca onestamente di trarne insegnamento.
You can find the pretentious, you can find the traitor, people who whisper and people who shout, people who squander and people who die. You can find people who trust, you can find people who suspect, people who go to war, people who keep silent and people who plot. Ponder, my friend, reflect on it for a moment, and try honestly to learn a lesson from it.	Ritrovi il presuntuoso ritrovi il traditore Chi mormora e chi grida chi sperpera e chi muore Ritrovi chi ha fiducia ritrovi chi sospetta Chi va a fare la guerra chi tace e chi complotta. Ragiona amico mio riflettici un momento E cerca onestamente di trarne insegnamento
You have to agree that, inexorably, nothing is left of all those people, and those who lived with Titus and Trajan are all six feet under, together with Domitian. Ponder, my friend, reflect on it for a moment, and try honestly to learn a lesson from it.	Tu devi convenire che inesorabilmente Di tutta quella gente non è rimasto niente E quelli che han vissuto con Tito e con Traiano Son tutti sotto terra insieme a Domiziano. Ragiona amico mio riflettici un momento E cerca onestamente di trarne insegnamento
Then look around you, observe the living world, observe it extensively, it will be very informative. You'll see that nowadays there are people who	Poi guardati d' attorno osserva il mondo vivo Osservalo ampiamente sarà molto istruttivo Vedrai che al giorno d'oggi c'è chi ama e chi fa guerra

love and people who make war,
people who cry and people who make merry,
people who die and people who bury.
Ponder, my friend, reflect on it for a moment,
and try honestly to learn a lesson from it.

And then you'll understand that there is no way out
if you want to make your life worth something.
I'm not saying you have to live heroically,
but at least refuse to live for nothing.
Ponder, my friend, reflect on it for a moment,
and try honestly to learn a lesson from it.

Chi piange e chi fa festa chi muore e chi sotterra.
Ragiona amico mio riflettici un momento
E cerca onestamente di trarne insegnamento

E allora capirai che non c'è via d'uscita
Se vuoi dare un valore a tutta la tua vita
Non dico che tu debba campare eroicamente
Ma almeno rifiutare di vivere per niente.
Ragiona amico mio riflettici un momento
E cerca onestamente di trarne insegnamento

EATING FROGS

In the previous two chapters I showed you that starting/opening a business is not a difficult endeavour and also that buying a first investment property is not difficult at all.

Both things require you to do many boring things (paperwork, research, administration); both things will require a big upfront investment in time, savings, effort; both will require a good level of self-discipline to persist over a course of action for years and years.

This is exactly the reason why many people, **even if they can, won't do those things**.

It's not the fear of failure or of being judged; it's certainly not the difficult nature of implementing these plans; it's not the lack of specialised knowledge. These are all excuses that people tell themselves (and possibly believe) to mask a very simple fact:

Nobody likes to do boring or unpleasant stuff.

One of the most accomplished salespeople in the world, Brian Tracy, wrote a whole book on the subject. The title, reported here below in a font-size representative of the importance of the idea is:

EAT
THAT
FROG

If you really didn't like to eat frogs but you were in a prison where, each day, you have to eat a frog alive otherwise you might face torture, what do you do?

- Eat the frog late in the evening, after thinking the whole day about it
- Eat it at lunch time
- Eat it early in the morning, so it's out of the way.

That book, which is about procrastination and doing things you don't like, especially as a standard salesperson (cold calling, prospecting, getting rejected), suggests doing the most difficult things early in the morning – or as soon as possible.

It's amazing how, by following some simple advice, some STANDARD advice, you can generate enough wealth to live a comfortable life and, potentially, stop working in the future.

Many people follow the dream of quick money, magic solutions, success, and fame. These things can happen but are statistically irrelevant and there are always some untold stories: special talents, dedication since a young age to a specific skill, luck in getting the right numbers, dubious connections, or sheer genius.

If you're reading this book, it's quite likely that you haven't studied science non-stop for the last twenty years, that you haven't played and trained in football five hours a day for the last twenty years, and that you don't have any special connection with local politicians.

Well, my friend, you still have hope, as has been demonstrated in the previous pages.

THE VERT

I've been inline skating since the age of fourteen, at first just to go around and explore the city and later, as my skills and courage grew, to do more and more tricks. One of the most spectacular things you can do when inline skating is jumping off the halfpipe, which indeed is a very good metaphor for life.

It doesn't matter how prepared you are, how many people you watch jumping, how many wrist, elbow and knee protectors you wear. When you're there, on the edge of the vert, the only way to get to the other side is to:

- Focus
- Jump
- Land in the right position
- Manage and ENJOY the speed
- Try to get to the other side in one piece

otherwise it will really hurt.

The vert or a skate park can really be a metaphor for life (as can many sports). You'll just skate along for years and learn nothing if you don't try new things regularly.

Regular exercise can only bring you so far and, only by taking calculated risks and wearing the right protection, you can improve and eventually get to jump off the vert, make a 'soul grind', and so on.

It's very important to have someone to show you what to do, which technique works and to give you some encouragement; better still if you are surrounded by people that are also trying to jump the vert so that you can encourage each other. You need to be in the game to try and win it.

Some people will be unlucky and, even if they had all their protection and prepared all they could, they will still fall, and may decide not to skate again. Some other people are naturally born to be stars and they will pick it up quickly.

In this book, we're trying to become good enough so that we can jump the vert and make it work (somehow) and, potentially, aspire one day to get to some international competition but, if you never jump, nothing will ever happen.

Jump and make it work.

MAKING AND BREAKING THE GRID

My wife is interested in graphic design and a few years ago she bought a book titled: 'Making and Breaking the Grid'. In graphic design there's a technique called the grid, where you use a grid system to put things in the right position to organise a website, a magazine, a newspaper and so on.

When designers start to make their first designs, it's important that they stick to certain principles and standards that are known to work. By copying what has already been done and mastering the understanding of the grid, even someone with no special artistic talent, can come up with some good layouts.

However, after you've practiced for weeks and months and produced dozens or even hundreds of layouts walking on a known path, you will start to hit a limit of what can be achieved.

Certainly, a possible approach in business and manufacturing is the one that pursues perfection: if you create systems that work perfectly, where there are virtually no errors, where everything has been optimised and what you do (a haircut, a cake, a GCMS instrument or an airplane) is always consistent, that can lead to massive success in itself because people like to buy products and services they can trust. Again, this is no magic wand: you just have to work hard, put the right processes in place and spend enough time on things to make them really good.

On the other hand, if you want to reach what I define as Level 4, you need to 'break the grid' and create your own playing field, with your own rules and your own laws. In simpler terms, you have to:

INNOVATE

Before you start writing down all your amazing ideas that could revolutionise the world, please be aware that:

- they are not amazing
- someone else has already started to implement them five to ten years ago
- they already have a working prototype
- you don't have the resources to make it
- you probably don't have the knowledge
- it would take you too long to get that knowledge or skillset if you don't already possess them

In this book, when I talk about making and breaking the grids and the systems, when I talk about innovation, I'm referring to:

- The grid/system that you know well: you have been working in this grid/system for the last four to ten years for eight hours a day
- In the sector that you know well and with your skills
- Where you clearly see space for innovation and improvement

This approach might seem under-ambitious and if you're the next Bill Gates or Elon Musk you probably can learn very little from it. However, for normal people with a standard set of skills, this is a good way forward:

- Specialise
- Find a niche
- Start a business and innovate as much as possible in something that you really do know well

LIFE AND BUSINESS QUOTES

Over the last decade, I've read a lot about business, selling, and negotiation amongst other things and, from each book, I got some good ideas, inspiration and practical advice. I've been writing down each good idea on a Word document to remind myself. Below you will find a list of selected quotations with some comments.

"Every solution breeds new problems" (Arthur Bloch)

Unless we get to the level of gods, where we can create matter and energy from the vacuum, there will always be new problems. The survival of the human race is the ultimate goal and, it does not matter how many ingenious solutions we find, there will always be new problems to solve to keep humanity moving forward.

In business terms this means that opportunities are virtually infinite, from energy optimisation, to quantum computers, from more sustainable food to teaching services.

There's a lot to do if we want our species to survive... loads to do, forever.

"No problem is insoluble in all conceivable circumstances" (Isaac Asimov)

This is strictly connected to the previous quote. While there are always new problems, they can all be solved if we take (or if it was possible to take) into consideration all possible circumstances and variables.

This comes from a novel by the sci-fiction novel writer Isaac Asimov 'The Last Question' where a supercomputer is asked how entropy can be solved and the universe be saved from its cold destiny.

"The world is full of money. Some of it has my name on it. All I have to do is collect it." (Felix Dennis)

We have already discussed this.

"Make sure you are hiring only A-players. Delegate, even if to B-players, they will become A-players under the right conditions."

This is one of those strange sentences. Ideally, you only want to get A-players but, unless you are already running a substantial company, how do you do it? In real life you are stuck with B and C-players that, under the right circumstances, will become amazing assets for your business.

"Tomorrow you may want to persuade somebody to do something. Before you speak, pause and ask yourself: "How can I make this person want to do it?""

In business and life it's always about how you can align your interests with someone else's interests.

"The other person cares about what he or she wants. Who cares what your company desires? Talk about what they want!"

Same as above, focus on the other person.

"There is nothing else that so kills the ambitions of a person as criticisms from superiors. I never criticize anyone. I believe in giving a person incentive to work. So I am anxious to praise but loath to find fault. If I like anything, I am hearty in my approbation and lavish in my praise."
"One way to break into someone is to ask him for advice, for a lecture, for experience in admiration."
"We are interested in others when they are interested in us."
"Remember people's names and LISTEN to what they have to say." (Dale Carnegie)

All these quotations come from Carnegie's 'How to win friends and influence people', a classic read.

Start early in the morning, go to sleep early at night

This is mostly true and there is also a logic behind it.

If you wake up at 7:30, get to your main job by 9:00, and then work most of the day at someone else's dream, what you are basically doing is using the best part of your energy to make someone else's dream a reality. By the time you get back home it's 18:00, you want to eat something, do some stuff of your own choice, but you have, at best, four hours maximum left to work on your own project, after a tiring day at work.

In my case, I used to split the work for my own company: one-third in the morning between 7:00 and 8:00/8:30 and two-thirds in the evening. However, the real bonuses are weekends and holidays: you decide the price to pay and then you pay it.

Read, read and read

You must learn more and more, you must read more and more. But it's also important **what** you read and learn. If you read many books written by monks in 1500 AD it's going to be very difficult to use that knowledge for any business related activity. On the other hand, if you read the latest information and study the market for waste disposal or virtual reality, then you might get lucky and find some interesting information.

Turnover is vanity, profit is sanity, but cash is reality

Once your business has been established, improve your margins and MAKE MONEY.

Luck = Preparation x Opportunity

This is one of my favourites. Except for some very rare cases, luck does not exist alone, but is always a mix of preparation and opportunity.

If you're the owner of a factory producing face masks or hand sanitiser, you're probably doing a lot of money right now thanks to the COVID-19 pandemic.

Go back some years and who would really want to specialise in face masks production or hand sanitiser? Most people were still looking at cryptocurrencies while someone, unknowingly, was preparing to get lucky.

Therefore, to go beyond Level 2, you need a viable business. A business that focuses on a certain specific field and permits you the preparation. The opportunity is, often, out of your control. You can position yourself to take some good opportunities, but that is about it.

Some massive opportunities I see now are quantum computers, CRISPR, genetic medicine, waste-to-energy sector, climate change adaptation, work from home services, to mention a few.

Buy when there's blood in the streets, even if the blood is your own.

Unless the stock market or the value of the assets is at a very high price! You really want to buy based on price and value rather than on perceived value and panic.

Be positive, happy, smile, radiate positivity. A man without a smiling face must not open a shop.

How many times have you been into a shop to then decide: "never again"? People buy from people they like.

Give information as a question

You can either say:
- "This is the best solution / this is how you should do according to my experience"
OR
- "Did you know about this solution? Have you ever heard of such and such technology?"

You really want your customer to feel enabled to say: "This was my choice", "I decided to buy".

Every night write down the list of things you want to achieve the following day

Lists of things to do are important, you really do need a plan, otherwise nothing will even happen.

And then, to conclude this list, more pearls from "How to win friends and influence people":

"Let the other person save face."
"Use encouragement. Make the fault seem easy to correct."
"Make the other person happy about doing the thing you suggest."
"Forget about the benefits to yourself and concentrate on the benefits to the other person."
"Be empathetic. Ask yourself what it is the other person really wants."
"The only way to get the best of an argument is to avoid it."
"Show respect for the other person's opinions. Never say, "You're wrong.""
"Let the other person do a great deal of the talking."
"Let the other person feel that the idea is his or hers."

All of this can be summarised with a few words: be a decent person, who is genuinely interested in helping others and uses his own skills to produce goods and services that are useful to other people. Be interested in people, not because of their money, but because of them, and enjoy the process of making money, living life, and learning about the world as your business moves forward.

Interphase
(the practice)

*Numbers,
practice and
mistakes to avoid*

Facts are stubborn things; and whatever may be our wishes, our inclinations, or the dictates of our passions, they cannot alter the state of facts and evidence.
John Adams

MORTGAGES

Since an important part of your financial independence will depend on properties, I really felt the need to spend some more time explaining how this part works in further detail. As always, the numbers and examples I will use are specific to the UK market, so you will have to translate them into your specific country in order for them to work.

Types of mortgages (1)

There are mainly two types of mortgage:
- Fixed rate mortgages
- Variable rate mortgages (with two subtypes: standard variable and trackers)

A fixed rate mortgage will usually be fixed for a number of years and will then change to a variable rate. A variable rate one instead will just follow the central bank's interest rate, plus whichever margin the bank decides to apply.

The advantage of a fixed rate is that you know **how much you must pay each month**; the advantage of a variable rate is that it usually charges **lower interests**.

If you Google: 'mortgage comparison', 'find a mortgage' and similar terms, you'll find websites that can help you to see what kind of mortgages you can choose from. I prefer to deal with fixed interest rates since what we have been experiencing since 2008 is an anomaly: interest rates that are close to zero and, in some countries, even negative. Below, you can see a graph showing the interest rate of the Bank of England in the last two hundred years.

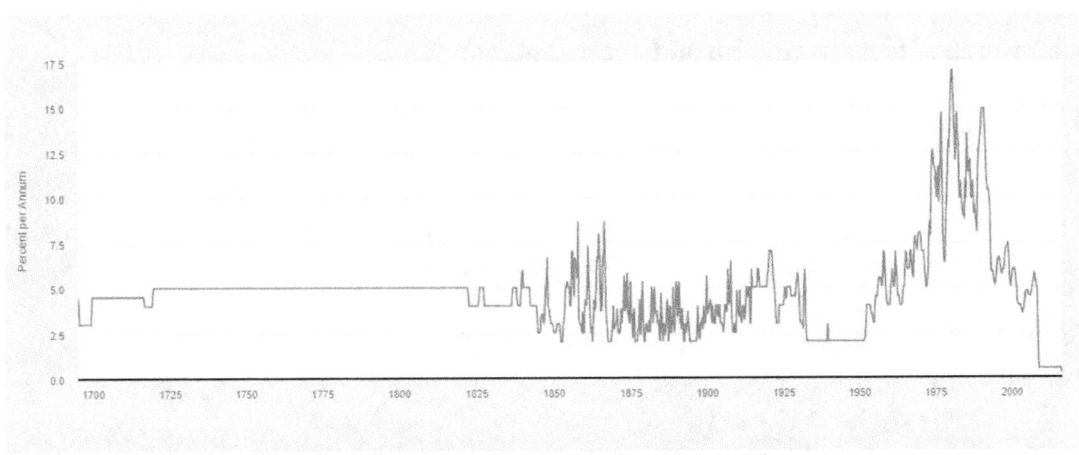

Source: Source: Bank of England – 300-year History

Now, given that we are at rock bottom and that, at some point, interest rates will increase (and might even increase fast), do we really want to take that extra risk to save a few thousand pounds? My answer is no, but I could be wrong and interest rates may stay low for the next twenty years. Moreover, the more you research about interest rates the more you realise that nobody really knows.

Types of mortgages (2)

Another distinction is between:

- Repayment mortgage
- Interest only

On a repayment mortgage you repay the money you have borrowed AND the interest; on an interest only mortgage you only pay the interest and, at the end of the mortgage, you have to pay the capital you borrowed (so basically you buy time by paying the interests).

The first type of mortgage is the one that most people have and like; the second type makes sense if: you need the cash flow, the house prices are rising and rising fast and you know that you will have the money or the situation to pay off the house at the end of the term.

Term of the mortgage

This refers to the duration of the mortgage, for example you can take out a twenty-five year mortgage, a forty year mortgage or a fifteen year mortgage. Usually there's a fixed term within which the amount you pay is fixed and then becomes a variable term.

Interest rates, fees, fixed term and overpayments

The bank charges you an interest rate and this is where a mortgage broker can be very useful since they get access to more deals.

The bank might also charge you some fees to set up the mortgage (thousands of pounds) or it might not, again the mortgage broker can help.

Also, fixed mortgages have a 'fixed term', which is a period during which you pay a penalty if you:

- Pay off the mortgage
- Sell the house and pay off the mortgage
- Overpay more than is allowed – usually 10%

This is so that the bank can be sure to make some money before you decide that you have won the lottery or move to a better deal.

Some mortgages allow you to make overpayments of up to 10% of the value of the loan. Let's say that you have a £140,000 mortgage, if your mortgage allows overpayments, you can bring that amount down by £13,000 in the first year, usually without incurring any overpayment charges. This has some massive benefits in terms of the amount of interest that you pay. We'll look at this later.

Finally, a mortgage broker has got some detailed market knowledge about which bank is more likely to accept your application and this means that you won't get rejected. If you get rejected for a loan once or twice, this appears on your credit score and then you will get rejected more. So avoid stupid mistakes and get a broker.

Remortgaging

As you don't want to stick with the same energy supplier so that you don't get overcharged, you also do NOT want to stick with the same bank once the fixed term is over.

If you have a fifteen year mortgage, for the first five years you might have a fixed interest rate and then it will change to a variable rate, usually higher than the fixed one.

Due to **laziness**, many people keep the same mortgage after the fixed term and get charged thousands in additional interests. It is insane and it happens all the time because of... guess what?

Paperwork!

Never let paperwork stop you from making money.

Now, things change quickly on the internet and putting a link in a book seems naïve, however there are some tools which are just too good not to be shared. If by the time you are reading this book the link does not work anymore just Google 'mortgage calculator' and 'mortgage overpayment calculator'. Here are the two links from an amazing website (Money Saving Expert) with a lot of interesting information and that I often use:

Mortgage calculator:
https://www.moneysavingexpert.com/mortgages/mortgage-rate-calculator/

Mortgage overpayment calculator:
https://www.moneysavingexpert.com/mortgages/mortgage-overpayment-calculator/

Go to these pages (or similar tools) and start getting your hands-on experience in how to use and forecast. An interesting example is the one that shows you how much money you can save by doing overpaying each month. Let's go through an example just to show you the power of overpayments.

Let's assume that we have:

- £133,000 left on your repayment mortgage
- A term of thirty-two years
- An interest rate of 2.44%
- A normal repayment of around £500
- And, on top of that, you start to repay £620 per month (the savings of Jenny and Xiaohui)

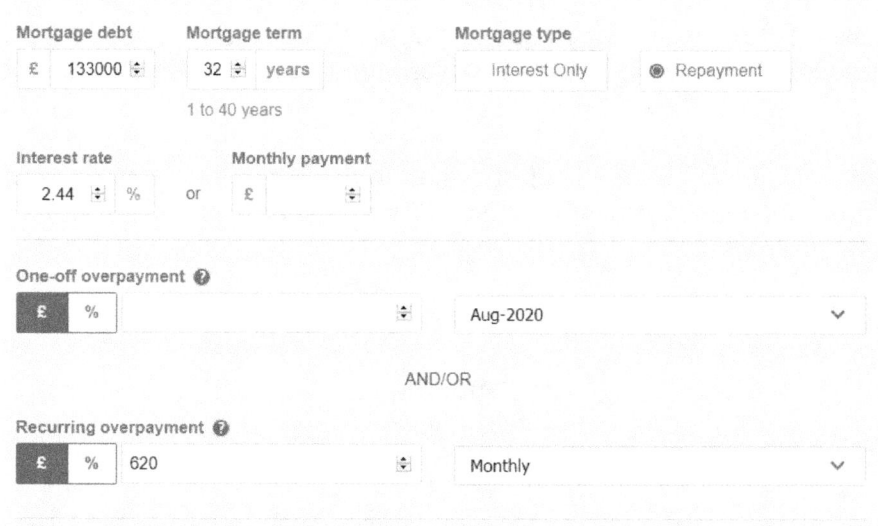

Screenshot from moneysavingexpert.com

The result, in terms of saved interest and repayment of the houses are quite amazing.

All of a sudden you can pay off the mortgage in twelve years and save almost £40,000 on interest.

Overpaying would save you **£39,395** in interest alone, and mean you pay the debt off in full **20 years** & **7 months** earlier.

Normally you repay **£500** per month. If you regularly overpay £620, you'd be mortgage free **20 years** and **7 months** earlier. Your total payment over this period would be **£152,412**.

Your mortgage debt over time

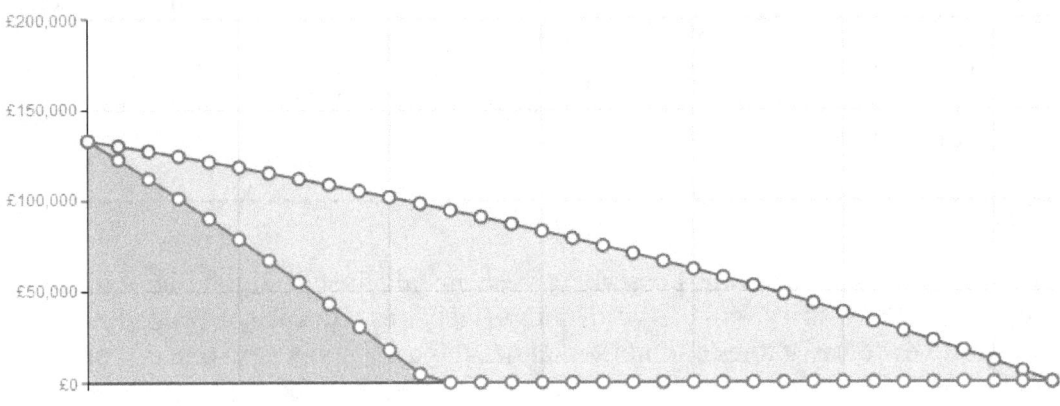

Screenshot from moneysavingexpert.com

Obviously, this is an over-simplification because:

- You will probably renegotiate the mortgage once the fixed term is over, and get a shorter mortgage, make some big overpayments and pay less interest.
- There will be times when you cannot pay that money and things might slow down.
- There will be times when you will have maxed out your overpayment allowance and you will have to wait so as not to incur any penalties.

Finally, overpaying the mortgage makes really sense in the first few years when, what you are really paying is **the interest rather than the principal** (the principal is the sum that you have borrowed), so you might decide to overpay 10% each year for the first few years and then renegotiate a better and shorter mortgage, or let it roll if you are confident that interest rates will stay low.

Exercise – Play with the mortgage repayment and overpayment calculator

Play around with these tools, explore the market, see what you can get from property websites and start working to buy your first home or your first buy-to-let.

KEEPING ORDER: PRACTICAL TIPS

As said many times, paperwork will literally kill you as you start and grow your business and wealth: books, papers, passwords, deadlines etc. will all become a mess. Here are some practical tips for you to follow.

Passwords

Just write them down, on a notepad, that you can hide somewhere, but please don't rely on memory or master passwords. Just write them down. If someone breaks into your house, they don't really care about your mail password, but they will care about your money and electrical goods. People who break into other people's houses aren't that bright.

Your PC

Give your PC a good clean, possibly a fresh install. Install a good antivirus software and some security tools. Avoid dodgy websites, illegal software downloads and I would even say games and non-essential things. This is now one of your main tools to make money, you want it to be fast, safe and protected.

Also, if you're working and at the same time on building your property portfolio AND your own business, I'd make separate accounts on your PC (User-Properties, User-Business, User-Improvement and Master-User) with the Master-User being the one who will be able to install/uninstall software for added security.

For each user create a folder which is synchronised with the Cloud so that all your non-strictly confidential files are backed up regularly and an email address. This is especially important for your properties and for your business.

For email addresses associated with properties, I decided to avoid names that show that we have more than one house. The story I tell all my tenants is: "This is our first house and, one day, we would really like to come back here. However, due to the work situation, we have to rent it out, so please take good care of it".

All of a sudden, you're not the greedy landlord anymore but you're a victim of a system that has obliged you to leave your beloved house: your tenants will like you more, won't be confrontational, will treat your house well AND, above all, they will not feel as if they're failing if they are much older than you. There is no need for them (or anybody else) to know about your wealth.

Also, in your property email account you probably want to create a **folder for each property** and, ideally, some subfolders to keep mortgage, tenants, legal and compliance matters separated and filed, not only in paper and in your synchronised folder but also in your email.

Obviously, using Outlook, Thunderbird or any email software, you can have a profile for each user which makes life easier.

Now that your PC is organised as a money-making platform, it should look something like this:

- User-Properties (Account)
    - Desktop -> One folder called 'Properties' with these subfolders
        - Property-1
            - Mortgage-papers
            - Legal
            - Tenants-Data
            - Ads-Photos-Descriptions
        - Accounting
- User-Business
    - Desktop -> One folder called 'Business' with some standard folders
        - Accounts
        - Marketing
        - Customers
        - Products
        - Website
        - Etc…

and so on. Just remember that your PC is a tool to make money, it is not a cinema!

Paper

Now that your passwords and PC are sorted, and before the tidal wave of paper comes in, go out and buy some folders, some containers for paper, a stapler and all the necessaries to keep paper organised. Don't do this later, do it now. You will receive, from now on, industrial quantities of paper, leaflets, terms and conditions, forms, etc. As soon as you get them, process them, throw away what you do not need, file what you need, move on.

You will also need a bookshelf and a place to put everything and keep it tidy, a good layout for a bookshelf is one with squares since it makes it easier to organise the different sections. Your bookshelf will likely need the following sections:

- Tax returns: main job, business and rental properties
- Business: legal, accounting
- Business: marketing and various
- Properties: purchase deeds, surveys, results of the searches etc.
- Properties: tenants, contracts, gas/electricity certificates

- Properties: mortgage papers
- Personal development
- Current paperwork (associated with your current stuff: job, house, bills etc.)
- And if you live abroad…an archive of everything you have ever done and paid

In our case, this is easily 50-60 kg of stuff and, while we keep throwing away and thinning out every few months, it continues to grow.

Your mind

Last but not least, have a minimum of two notebooks. In one you'll write any idea of things that you can improve in your business. In the other, you'll write and delete the things you have to do today, this week or this month. Usually, you should start from micro-tasks such as:

- Write brochure on Product 24
- Link building for the website
- Review Section 4 of the User's Manual
- Order some fittings

But eventually you will get into the habit of working hard on things so you can be more general.

THE CREATOR

There is a song by Santigold, an American singer, called 'The Creator' that really explains this concept well, I strongly suggest you listen to it NOW. At one point it says:

> Sit tight I know what you are
> Mad bright but you ain't no star
> **Polish up 'til you make it gleam**
> Your M.O, I know what you mean

In business, in art and in life you must "Polish up 'til you make it gleam", there's no better way to say this. Whatever you do, you really need to spend the time, the energy, and the focus to make it gleam. What does this mean for business? Everything.

A few pages back we described how, in order to excel, you need to innovate. However, before you even try to innovate, you want to get as close as possible to a perfect execution of what you are already doing.

Appearances

Most businesses nowadays have a website and, having run a web design company, even for a short period of time, I cringe when I see people spending thousands of pounds on "stuff" for their business and, all of a sudden, getting very greedy when it comes to getting a proper website done.

It's true that some companies charge a fortune to make a website but nowadays, on a freelancer platform like Fiverr, you can easily find all the resources you need to get a decent website done. Now, this does NOT aim to be a book about web design, SEO or even marketing, but it's so important in the post-COVID world that we go into the nitty-gritty in the next section.

For now, just remember: if your website and your marketing material looks credible then, in the eyes of customers, you ARE credible. This obviously is not limited to a website but to your whole business.

If you want to buy a camera, would you buy it from a shop that just sells cameras, or are you more likely to buy it from a shop that has a sparkling section on their website, where they explain, free-of-charge how to use the camera?

If you want to get a pizza, do you get it from a place that gives you a homey feeling, where you can sit down in a warm environment with nice interiors, or from a place with the bare minimum, empty and poorly kept?

If you want to go to yoga classes, would you go to a teacher who is unkempt and in a place which is a bit tatty, or would you rather meet a friendly and tidy teacher in a clean place.

If you send an invoice, do you send it in a standard template in Word or you spend some time to make it look as professional as it seems? If you're making your brochures, do you give a number and a publication date and put in place a document control system (even a basic one) or not? With your quotations, do you send terms and conditions or not? Have you checked the grammar on your website? On your marketing material? Is your packaging fit for purpose? Is your office clean and tidy? Is your workshop presentable?

It doesn't matter what you think about 'being' vs 'appearing'; from a philosophical perspective, in business you need to appear, because that's the first thing a customer can judge your level of dedication from, before buying the service/product.

Quality and service

The next obvious ones are quality and service. You want your products to be the highest possible standard that you can achieve and your service to be as good as possible.

STOP!

At this very moment, many of you will be thinking: "OK, this is bloody obvious, are you trying to lengthen your book by writing obvious stuff?". Then let me ask you:

- How many times were you disappointed after purchasing a good?
- How many times were you disappointed after purchasing a service?
- How many times when walking in a shop, visiting a website, looking at a product or thinking about a service you **have thought of all the things that can be improved**?

Personally, thousands of times!

From sloppy customer service to brochures with two sentences and three spelling errors, from untidy business premises to just rude behaviour. The list goes on forever and you sometimes wonder how are these people still in business?

All these businesspeople aren't stupid, certainly many are not doing it on purpose and, compared with the majority of people, at least, they are doing something. However, while you're worrying about your next order, struggling with paperwork and deadlines, dealing with your personal life and, at the same time, chasing customers for payments it is **fully understandable but completely unjustifiable** that quality and service might suffer.

KEEP THIS IN MIND

And, put a note for yourself to review this very paragraph when you have been actively running your business for four months.

Everybody is looking for fancy and amazing ideas, when most can't be bothered to do the bare minimum. Let's start from there before worrying about complicated issues.

<u>Delivery and post-purchase service</u>

If your business involves shipping items, pay attention to the packaging: a big package for a little item and the customer will think: "this is wasteful", a small package for a fragile good and the customer will think: "it's broken". Branded packaging will also make you appear more professional to the customer.

Finally, always remember to keep helping the customer even after the purchase, even if it's a hassle and a difficult customer.

<u>In summary</u>

Present your offering as well as possible, deliver quality products and service, make sure it arrives in one piece and keep the contact and the service going even past the point of purchase.

WEBSITE AND MARKETING

This section is really important, and most of you need it, yet many will feel that it's too technical.

Let's clear some doubts first. You want to focus on your own business, you don't want to become a web designer or a graphic designer. When you need a new boiler you call a gas engineer, you don't spend twelve months learning how to install and service a boiler. Unless your business requires you to really understand the nuts and bolts of how the web works, my advice is to read a lot about how things should be done but then ask a professional to implement it.

Buying your first domain and hosting

You can get free websites with addresses like www.something.somethingelse.com, however, since a domain name costs around £10 per year it would be crazy not to register one. If you Google 'register domain name' you get various options to do so. After you have a domain name, like www.thenameofmyamazingbusiness.com, you need to choose a hosting service, which is where your website will go. The domain name is only the name, the hosting is the remote computer or server where the files of your website will be located.

When you choose your domain name, think long and carefully:

- Will you always service a local area? www.sheffieldbarbers.co.uk might be good for barbers in Sheffield
- Will you sell materials worldwide? Then you want something short and memorable.com
- Are there some key markets that you serve worldwide? Then register the .com but also the .it, .fr, .es, and so on

In regard to the hosting, as a start-up company, a shared hosting with a few GBs of disk space, five email addresses, a control panel (ideally cPanel) and support for PHP/MySQL (or any other database) is enough, which means no more than £100 per year but possibly less[14].

Getting the material together

At this point, don't worry too much about the design of your website, a designer will think about it. Focus on the content of the website.

---

[14] This might seem too specific for a book of this kind, but hey! I'm telling you how to make money.

For example, if you have a business that offers pest control or rat removals, you probably want to write detailed material about:

- The problem: pests, rats and other things you can take care of
- Why it occurs
- What is your service (in detail) with pictures
- What is your process to remove the rats
- What is the price range

Many people get stuck at this point because this is a frog! To eat! Uncooked and in the morning.

To have a chance to appear on Google, your website must be reputable and have informative and useful content so, if you want to be found on Google, you must play the game or not bother at all.

Once you have written several pages of material, you have to take pictures and even make some videos. The more material you put together the better.

Contact an expert

At this point you have probably spent £100 for hosting and domain and thirty-plus hours putting together the material for brochures, website etc. What do you do now? That depends mainly on your sector. If selling online is important for your business, then find a freelancer, pay anything between £200 and £1,000 and get your website sorted out properly.

Since you will be paying an expert, you want a job done properly which basically means:

- Your website should work well on all major browsers (Chrome, Firefox, Safari, Edge)
- At various resolutions
- On various devices (mobile, tablet, desktop)
- It should load fast: https://developers.google.com/speed/pagespeed/insights/
- And there should be no missing links, wrong numbers, wrong email addresses and so on

Also, you probably want to do some basic Search Engine Optimisation and there are plenty of guides on the internet.

Which platform?

There are some platforms called Content Management Systems (CMS) which allow you to edit the content of your website without knowing the code. While at the beginning this might seem like a good idea, it usually isn't since you will end up paying an expert to fix problems associated with the complexity of these systems and they are bulky and tend to be slower. Unless your business really needs a CMS, don't use solutions such as WordPress, Joomla etc.

Promotion and tracking

Now that you have a working website with various pages, a few social media profiles as well as LinkedIn, and all the standard stuff, it's time for promotion. Hopefully, if you have spent enough time and eaten many frogs, Google will work its magic and slowly you will see visits going up. A very good source for SEO advice is https://backlinko.com/. As always, no magic but a lot of hard work and common sense.

Software choices

As you are proceeding, you're already starting to see the costs creep up. Certainly, you can start virtually with a free website, free domain name, make your own website or use a pre-made template), however, as your business starts to grow you might need the edge to win against competitors and this is where the software comes in.

For almost every paid software there are free alternatives. Most businesses do not need specialised software and the free alternatives are enough. On the other hand, in some industries, saving money on software is sheer folly since although you might save money on the software, the customers will certainly save money by not buying from you as a result of your sub-optimal presentations, marketing and service.

I have seen some multi-million pound companies running on free software and, while they are still working: the amount of man-hours spent on unusable software as well as the sub-optimal results that can be obtained make it a real mystery for me to understand why business owners don't not invest in software when necessary.

PERSONAL DEVELOPMENT

With all the flurry of buying properties, managing mortgages, working on your website, delivering high quality goods and services while saving money and living a modest life you might forget (this is a remote possibility of course) to keep learning!

As you start this journey you will start to seek more and more knowledge regarding:

- tax matters and personal finance
- home improvements, property management, tenant management and even DIY
- your business, your specific activity, your specific product
- everything else that surrounds the business and the properties

Luckily, compared with twenty years ago, you can basically learn everything online (even how to make money), there are universities offering free courses and paid courses. Websites such as Course Era and Udemy offer courses on many topics for very good prices. YouTube tutorials, websites on specific topics and much more are getting better and better.

All the information you will ever need is out there, basically free, so we do not have any excuse not to learn and improve.

What else is there to say?

NOTICE: EVERYTHING TO THIS POINT IS PERFECTLY FEASIBLE

Level 1 and Level 2 – To do list

Find your first job

1. Decide that you want to make money and analyse your starting point
2. Make a plan
3. Keep in mind the Pay/Career/Location matrix: find where you can make a living
4. Read about finding your first job, interviews, CVs, cover letters
5. Polish up your CV and cover letter, and subscribe to job search engines
6. Apply to every position that you can find and get the job
7. If necessary/possible move abroad or to any place …
8. …where you can start saving money
9. Open a separate bank account for your savings

Improve your job

1. If your job does not give you new skills/insight, look for a better job
2. At the same time, study to get into a specific sector/trade: have a self-improvement plan
3. Get the new job, with higher pay and, above all, higher levels of specialisation
4. Continue to save money, find love, discuss this plan with your partner
5. You both decide that you want to become financially independent
6. Optimise your expenses
7. Save more money

Buy your first home

1. Study the area, talk with mortgage brokers, read about buying, selling and investing
2. Think as an investor, negotiate hard and buy your first house
3. Rent out a room straight away to someone you are happy to live with
4. Optimise your expenses even more: renegotiate everything
5. Continue working hard, studying a lot and saving money
6. Bring that mortgage down quickly, overpay, save more money

Start your side activity

1. Decide that you want to start making money on the side, choose something realistic
2. Work on website, marketing, products, delivery, logistic etc. as a tax-free/sole trader
3. Work, work and work: polish it up until you make it gleam

4. If necessary, move from sole trader to a limited company
5. The company must be self-sustaining
6. You have to continue studying and learning

Buy your first investment property

1. Do your research on taxes, what's the best way to buy etc.
2. Do all the due diligence and negotiate hard
3. Buy it, fix it and rent it out as soon as possible
4. Stabilise the income, learn how to manage it, do it slowly and well
5. Grow some basic wealth

DO IT!

Level 3

*More properties,
more business,
more connections,
more YOU*

Build your own dreams, or someone else will hire you to build theirs.
Farrah Gray

Chapter 9 – The Junction

We are now halfway through our journey of drudgery, savings, hard work and consistency that will make you a small fortune and put you and your business in a position to make a lot of money if the right opportunities come into your life.

At this point in the book I'm assuming that the reader, by saving money on a daily basis, investing their money first in a house and then in a buy-to-let, starting their own small size business while keeping their main job and improving themselves are starting to face some dilemmas and are at a junction.

- Should I focus on closing the mortgages I have?
- Should we invest in yet another property?
- Should I invest in the business?
- Should I move to another country?
- Do I need some more specialised knowledge?
- Is all this work worth it?

Let's clear some important points before moving on, both for intellectual coherence but also to be able to fully understand why I will suggest a certain course of action.

Your properties

When you read books and articles about how to make money in the property market, creating a property portfolio and generating a passive income from rental properties so you can stop working and live the life you have always dreamt of, very often everything seems too easy, too rosy to be true, too smooth. The reason why the readers get that feeling is because those books are usually selling a dream rather than telling the facts.

In the worst cases they're clearly scamming wannabe property investors, selling expensive courses in different tiers by self-appointed property gurus; in the best cases they're starting from the wrong assumptions or are generalising assumptions which are not necessarily true.

We're clever enough to understand that if someone wants to charge us hundreds of pounds for a day training, it's probably a scam. On the other hand, it can be confusing to see why some models work so well in theory, but they seem impossible in reality.

Factors that affect house prices

It's important to understand the economics and the politics behind property price growth.

First of all, there's **population growth**, which is what people think is the main reason for house prices growth. If in the same space you put 10% more people (through migration and natural growth) house prices will increase. Obviously, if that 10% is mainly unskilled labour, they won't buy a property but will have to rent forever or for a very long time and that will benefit mainly landlords who serve that market. For this reason, despite the rhetoric, many politicians who are also landlords like immigration and population growth. On the other hand, if that 10% is made up of highly qualified professionals, many of them might decide to settle down and buy a house, pushing prices up. This, in turn, will be welcomed by house builders and landowners.

However, the world is not a static place and luckily, every now and then, some ambitious house building programs are implemented to build affordable housing. So, as the population grows so does the **number of houses**, which is the second factor.

A third, extremely important factor, is the **availability of mortgages**. If banks start to make lending more difficult (for example because of the massive unemployment feared at the time of writing as a result of the COVID-19 pandemic), then less people have access to the credit or the loans get smaller, which means that sellers will have to accept lower prices or much longer times to sell.

A fourth factor is represented by **economic shocks**: during a recession, when people lose jobs and default on their mortgages, houses are sold at auctions and, with limited buyers, banks and institutions try to cut the losses and accept lower prices.

All this simply means one thing: forecasting house prices in the medium term is quite difficult. In the short term it might be easy, because you're seeing what's happening; in the long term it's relatively easy because you can observe some macrotrends and make an educated bet: growing population, climate change, political instability in certain areas, will mean increased migration and development in other areas.

So, our real problem is not to predict what will happen in the next year or in the next thirty years, but to know what will happen in the next three to fifteen years which is, incidentally, the timeframe most of us are really interested in.

Models that don't work

In some books about property investment, the author might say something along these lines:

In the current market house prices grow 6% year on year; this means that if we buy a property for £100,000 today, after five years of 6% increases each year the value will be £134,000 and you will have made £34,000....

...except that...

House prices don't necessarily grow year on year at 6%. They might grow at 2% for three years in a row, then lose 1%, then grow 2%. All of a sudden, the model falls apart, at least in the medium term.

Eventually, house prices tend to grow and grow substantially and investing in properties almost always makes financial sense. But if you're in your forties and start investing today and your country/area is entering a phase of stagnation then it might take fifteen years for things to turn out the way you imagined. For this reason, if you're in your twenties or early thirties, you should really have a **sense of URGENCY** when it comes to investing in properties: it will take time, it may take a long time, or even take a *very* long time for the investment to give you a good return.

If this is the case in your country/time then, all of a sudden, you cannot 'leverage' the existing property, which means that you can't take money out (equity release) of a property to finance the purchase of another one which means that you're now basically relying on your savings to finance the deposits.

Following the 2008 crisis, lending criteria have become very strict so, for example, for a buy-to-let you need at least a 25% deposit which, on a £100,000 is £25,000 which will take our friends Xiaohui and Jenny three and a half years to save by saving £620 per month.

On the other hand, if you're in an emerging market and house prices are increasing, then the wisdom coming from books written in periods of high interest rates, high inflation and high house price growth, is all still valid. Personally, I don't see this happening in western Europe anytime soon: there might be modest growth, some cities might experience some 'booms' but the Old Europe is stuck between -2% and +3% for a very long time.

So, what's next?

Well, the answer is: it depends. If you're in a market that is growing (i.e. India) I would probably focus more on investing in properties and establish a portfolio of four to eight properties by:

- Buying at a low price
- Waiting for the value of the house to grow
- Releasing the equity
- Buying the next house

If the house and rent prices are growing and you are saving money, you could buy a property every two years and then every year.
On the other hand, if you're in a stable market where things are looking flattish, then I would stop at the third or fourth property and then use the rest of the time and

resources to either invest in growing the business, paying off the mortgages, invest in something else, or a combination.

This is a well-needed dose of realism since, many of you that will read this book in a post-COVID market will probably not experience accelerated house prices growth for at least a few years, so telling stories of wealth done with schemes that will not work is, I think, unethical.

But I may be wrong!

Changing attitudes

There is also another factor to consider: changing attitudes and changing political landscape. The house price in the Western world has been mainly fuelled by baby boomers and by some generations that had a lot of wealth to invest in material goods. As the newer generations start to have their own wealth, will they invest in properties? Will they buy more than one property pushing prices up? Will 'generation rent' eventually vote in political leaders that will fix rental prices, or build many houses?

These are just some passing thoughts and it's very difficult to know for sure what will happen, however, this is the reason you need to diversify and you should not only rely on the 'lazy' properties. I call them lazy because, when you get £600 per month from a house just because you have put your name against it and some deposit, that's lazy, pure and simple.

Properties…but not only!

For many people, the attractiveness of owning real estate depends on the fact that you don't need any specialised knowledge. OK, some understanding of how tax and mortgages work is needed, but that is promptly acquired. Also, properties are 'easier': it's one thing to run a shop, manage suppliers, manage customers, do this and do that; it's another thing to get a call every few months because something has broken and then make a call to ask someone else to fix it. Come on, it's not difficult.

If you rely only on properties for your wealth strategy, you're not diversifying even if you buy different kinds of properties. You might invest in commercial and residential, but the concept is the same: extracting value for almost no work.

So, while it's essential that you have a property portfolio, it is also important not to be reliant on it. Imagine the hypothetical situation where you rearrange your properties/wealth so that you end up with five properties and each one is giving you a net income of £200 (after you pay taxes, account for maintenance etc.), which basically means you earn £1,000 per month from properties.

In many parts of the world, you can live quite well for £1,000 per month so, you might think to:

- rearrange the properties/mortgages to get as much cash as possible
- move somewhere where life is cheap
- spend a few months at a time in different countries so as to avoid becoming a permanent resident - you're liable on your worldwide income when you become a permanent resident in one specific country, keep this in mind!

For example, you may decide to spend a few years between Malaysia, Thailand, Myanmar, Cambodia and Vietnam. That sounds like a dream, doesn't it?

Indeed, when my wife and I went to Thailand for a month and stayed put on the island of Koh Chang, our life was amazing, and our expenditures were minimal, so it is feasible.

However, what happens when something doesn't go according to plan? What happens when the boiler breaks in property no. 3 and your tenants have cold water in their shower? Do you try to fix it under warranty in the middle of the winter with waiting times of one week OR **you do the right thing**, pay someone to fix it the same day and then try to sort out the warranty? What happens when a tenant is struggling with the rent for no fault of their own? Do you evict them to pay for your lifestyle OR you try to work out a solution?

What I'm trying to say is that properties should not be seen as the main source of income (unless you have twenty-plus properties) but more of a complement, a bonus, a value reserve, a safe asset, basically something where you and your tenants together throw value in so that, **at a much later date**, you can take it out.

We will talk later about some other concepts such as Capital Gain Tax, Income Tax, taxation on company profits etc. that will show you how, by using a limited company you can grow a portfolio of properties BUT, even in that case, do you really want to rely on one thing alone?

For this reason, what's important when you're at The Junction are the other two points of the strategy: your business and yourself.

Your business

This is where you want to focus most of your energies, time and money when you're at the junction, not in properties, UNLESS your business *are* properties (i.e. you are a builder or a trader who can really add value through the work you and your team do on a property).
When you started your business, you probably did it because you wanted to be your own boss, you had some good ideas to implement, you knew how to do things bet-

ter and you wanted to show yourself and eventually others that you were right. Except that, once you got into the game you realised that, while you might be much better at some things, you lacked other skills or resources and you don't have the time, money or energy to acquire them.

> Welcome to the real world of business, marginal increments and more hard work than you would ever had imagined was possible!
> And it was your choice!

Obviously, your business, is also your best lottery ticket. It's not by working for someone else that you're going to get a net worth of a few million pounds. Some high paid managers actually get there, but how many? Also, it's not by collecting an additional £50 of rent per month that you'll become a millionaire.

Your best shot at making money, real money, is through your business, but you must experience busyness alongside.

Business and Busyness

As a native Italian speaker, I find the English language fascinating. Italian certainly is a much more prolific language and can express complexity much better than English can. On the other hand, English has a way of being so direct, so simple, and yet complete, that Italian will never have. Try to translate a technical document from English into Italian and keep the same layout: good luck! Italian needs double the words.

I think the words 'business' and 'busyness' are really the same. You don't have a business if you're not experiencing busyness, you cannot have a business and not be busy, and if you're not busy, well, you're not running your business properly.

Certainly, I'm not advocating to be busy for its own sake: it doesn't matter how many times you sweep the floor or you send the same email to the same person, past a certain point you might break the brush or alienate the customer.

What I'm saying, however, is that if you want a business, and if you want your business to grow, then you need to get busy, very busy...

Extremely busy eating frogs!

When you started this journey with this book, certainly you weren't expecting this. You were expecting perhaps some positive thinking, some secret formula to get rich, some mental gimmicks that will unlock your inner genius and so on.

Instead, you're here, reading a book by an author whose real name you ignore, that is constantly talking about saving, investing, marginal gains, self-improvement, hard-work and eating frogs. But the nice thing is that **this actually works**.

Very often, I have walked (and worked) into companies where the majority of the people were busy watching the screen, with tired eyes, slowly typing on the keyboard and basically doing nothing. Most of us have been guilty of that: not putting the energy, the passion, into what we do.

How many times have you been into a shop where the staff were just standing doing nothing? How many depressed and demotivated business owners have you met that were fidgeting with meaningless tasks and complaining that business wasn't good? Do you remember a few pages back where we talked about motivation? About the fact that there are plenty of things to do, to improve, to build, to invent, to streamline? Well, keep this well in mind:

> *As a business owner you should always be agonistically busy*

But let's look at some specific examples, just in case you're now thinking that this is just theoretical stuff. I will take examples from the business I know best, without giving too much away to respect their privacy.

Everything can be improved

You've now opened your shop or your business, and you're earning some money, but not much. You've passed the first psychological hurdle. You're sending some invoices, making some products, talking with your accountant once per month about money matters, selling some products and services. You're happy and you can proudly say to your friends and family: "My business is starting to show some results".

> Wait! Did you just think: "How did we get there?". Go back a few chapters and re-read the relevant sections but also continue reading onward.

On the other hand, you know very well that your full-time job pays you £2,500 a month every month while, your business could make you only £500 a month as things stand. You're working around twelve hours per day or more, plus weekends and holidays. You're not doing this for the money, but you're doing this "for your business". Time goes on and on, sales improve a little bit, then there's a dip, then you're back to where you were one year ago and you start to wonder: "Is this worth it?".

You are, again, at The Junction. You were at the junction with properties when you had to decide if you want to invest in a third or fourth rental property or not. You're now at the junction with your business, possibly with your life, and with your personal development.

The junction is a funny place to be, it can make you laugh when you realise how absurd a place to be this is. This is the place where everything can happen: you might get a contract coming out of the blue and make your first big profit, you might get into depression and give up, you might decide to sell everything and go on a long holiday, or you might find a good property development and make a killing.

Going back to the half-pipe and inline skating analogy.

The first step was to prepare, then you jumped off the vertical wall (the vert), you somehow managed to stay in one piece but, you're stuck in the middle of a half-pipe, with your inline skates and you're struggling to get any higher and, incidentally, you knee MIGHT start to ache.

Depending on the situation, you might want to either:

- Slow down, in case you dislodge your knee (basically, do not burn out)
- Keep pushing if your knee (mental and physical state) is fine

So, let's look at how you can keep pushing.

<u>Sales are low, I'm not making enough money</u>

This is the main issue of most businesses: sales. We'll talk more about this later, but hey, this is the important bit. It doesn't matter if you have the best product, the best marketing, if you're always dressed and well-groomed, if you're a highly specialised person: if you don't sell you'll go out of business, that's it.
Remember this:

Price is what you pay, value is what you buy.

When I go online and order some expensive organic food, what I'm buying is the value of the fresh tasting vegetables, the idea to help local farmers, the return scheme for the cardboard box to decrease plastic pollution, and the convenience of having it delivered at home.

When my wife walks fifteen minutes in the rain to go to the local coffee shop, the value she is buying is the experience of being in a warm environment during the winter, the fact of being pampered by the waitress with chocolate muffins and a cappuccino, the environment around her.

When I go to the local skate shop to buy some new inline skates (and pay £20 more than if I bought them online) the value I'm getting is the know-how, the support I get if anything goes wrong, the professional advice and the hope that, by supporting the local shop, the inline skating community will re-emerge.

When you buy a course on material design from an online platform, the value you are getting is the fact that you can do it from home, that it's cheaper than a university degree, that it's specific, and, usually, that it's quite good.

I'm sure you see where I'm going with this.

What is the value that you offer? Why should your customers buy from you? What are you offering them? Are you only putting some very low prices out there and hoping that some business will come your way? If your only selling point is a 'low price', do you really think you can compete with mass production giants?

**Define your value, define what you offer,
define your Unique Selling Point (USP).**

It might simply be the level of service that you offer. If you work hard to always be welcoming, ready to listen, ready to help, always tidy, well-dressed, with immaculate premises and so on, customers might come in just to be in a nice environment. On a recent trip to Asia, while I loved the people and the culture and I really don't like to spend money at chain shops, after five days spent walking through some very dirty streets, all that I wanted was a clean and calm place, so I ended up literally escaping to an international chain shop because I knew that there were going to be certain standards there. Probably if I lived there longer, I would have got used to it, but there I was spending a lot of money to get some coffee in a clean environment. And I felt so guilty about it!

So, how does all of this relate to: money, sales, business and busyness? Let's look at some more specific examples.

<u>Improve your product and/or service</u>

- Is your product functional? Is it easy to use? Can you change something to make it better?
- Do customers tell you: "It's good but....."? If yes, then you really want to LISTEN and ACT on what comes after the "but", rather than resisting criticism and change
- Have you actually studied the competitors? I don't mean just knowing the names of your competitors to show you know the market but to really understand their products as if you had to sell them yourself.
- What about the design of your product? Does it look good? What can you do to make it look more professional?
- Can you create some add-on products easily? Can you improve the ease of use? Can you produce it for a better price?

If you are 100% happy with everything you have done so far, it's because you really don't like to eat frogs. Almost everything can be improved. Similar considerations go for the service:

- Can you make it better? Can you streamline the process? Have you got written and detailed procedures? Checkboxes? Lists?
- Are you welcoming customers in the right way? With the right attitude? Are you too pushy? Are you too relaxed? How do other people perceive you?
- Do you need extra knowledge? Where and when will you get it from? How long will it take? How will you manage in the meantime?
- Do you need some extra tools? When can you get them? Are you trying to buy quality via a tool or is it a real need?

<u>Improve your marketing</u>

- Are your brochures done professionally? Are you in a competitive field where presentation is very important? Do your customers mainly buy from the internet or catalogues?
- **Are you at the same level of the market leaders in terms of marketing and presentation? If not, why not?**
- Are your brochures, datasheets, catalogues, articles, press releases, business cards, website, social media pages AT LEAST as good as those of the market leaders?
- If your business depends on sales and marketing, can you afford to pay for those skills? Can someone help you at the beginning? Should you learn those skills yourself? Can you get help with photography, graphic design and similar?
- Are you trying to make a hundred page catalogue with Scribus or would it be better to pay for InDesign? Are you trying to take amazing pictures with your phone camera or with a professional camera?

Marketing takes a lot of effort, it really does, and that's why most people/companies don't want to do it. You need:

- To think about the content and your marketing strategy
- Create the material yourself
- Present the material in such a way that is appealing to people
- Distribute this content in many ways
- Measure, improve and repeat

So, we can clearly see that, unless you want to be condemned to mediocrity, as long as you run a business, you should be busy with these two main tasks:

Improve the quality/quantity of your products and services
Improve the quality/quantity of your marketing material and sales activities

This is what you really need to focus on. Remember 'The Creator' ("Polish up 'til you make it gleam")? That is your busyness: a constant cycle of improving products, services, sales and marketing. This means that, if while you are running your business you think: "I have nothing to do", "there's nothing more that can be improved", "I'm not busy at all", then you really need to check your mindset, your priorities and your motivations.

BUSINESS = BUSYNESS = BUSINESS

If you persist long enough in this process (months or even years), eventually you'll be at the point where the quality of your products, services, marketing and sales will be at a level so high that customers and money will start to flow in naturally. As you are naturally drawn to good electronics, good clothing, good restaurants, good tradesman etc., everybody can be naturally drawn to your business if you've worked hard to make it shine.

Yourself

Of the three elements of our strategy, this is the most important one: who you are, what you want, where you're going, and why. We talked about motivation and why you should or could do certain things, and we have also emphasised how you should always try to learn new things. However, let's try to understand why YOU should be the main focus of the strategy and how you can't reasonably expect to do only a little work on yourself and excel in property investment, business, and life at large.

<u>The life that never was</u>

When most people think about making money, they're thinking about the lifestyle it can obtain: the house with a sea view on the Mediterranean, the endless holidays, the multi-million pound yacht, the nights out partying among the stars and all those Hollywood-induced dreams that help actors and actresses make a fortune (and live those dreams) by selling those very dreams to people who will never be able to afford them.

During my career I have met hundreds, if not thousands, of businesspeople and, most of them, even the richest ones, are NOT living that life.

First of all, unless you inherit (not earn but *inherit*) substantial amounts of money, a cash-making business empire and a huge number of assets, you simply cannot afford too much extravagance. Even if you were earning, let's say £30,000 net per month from your properties and business, you would still be in no position to buy a superyacht with a crew of ten people; even if you could easily buy up large swathes of premium land, it would still take more than ten years of that level of income just to buy a £3.6 million house.

There can only be so many kings and queens in the world.

Secondly, even if you were to reach such a level of wealth (i.e. £20 million pounds in your bank account or more), starting from a standard background, would you really want to waste all of it buying expensive status symbol goods? Do you need a £20 million mansion? Do you need a superyacht? The answer is obviously a big fat NO.

There is, in all of this, a very important concept: if you're working hard to make money to buy superyacht, a £10 million mansion or to travel the world in extreme luxury, you're probably fooling yourself. If you're working hard because of a theoretical lifestyle that even people who own businesses which make substantial profits can't (or won't) afford, you're probably fighting a losing battle. To do that, you would need to get to Level 5, but because the growth from Level 2 to 3 and 3 to 4 and 4 to 5 is exponential, it gets harder and harder.

Moreover, when many people think about making money, they have in mind objectives which are diametrically opposed to the processes needed to make money in the first place. Let me explain.

The Objective: stop working, go on a long holiday, stop studying, put your feet up, buy an expensive car, a massive house, stay in five-star hotel, sail around the world, and so on. These are the things that many associate with money, riches, and wealth.

The Process: work extremely hard, forfeit your holidays, learn more and more, experience busyness, buy assets and not liabilities, live well within your means, reinvest, and explore the world while flying economy in the process. These are some of the processes that statistically will make you relatively wealthy.

How many stories have you heard of people winning tens, if not hundreds, of millions at the lottery who then ended up broke within a few years? How many people have had the luck to make a lot of money and then lost it all?

This is not because they weren't clever (or at least some of them), or because of some sort of evil nature of money (remember money is neutral), but simply because making money, managing money, protecting money and making even more money, are all things that require a certain level of knowledge, practice, personal skills, people skills, mindset, and so on.

That's why YOU are the centre of the strategy, not the properties that you buy, the business that you make, the products or the services, but YOU as a person, an individual, a mind, a creator of wealth.

Continuous improvement: specialised technical knowledge

There's one topic which we haven't explicitly discussed yet, but that's extremely important when it comes to making money: specific knowledge and specific skills. At the beginning of the book we underlined how it's important to specialise in a job where you can grow better and better at what you do and can improve your skills on a daily basis. This isn't because there are jobs which are more honourable than others, or because a certain job will give you a better status, those are side effects. The reason why a specialised job is important is because it gives you access to:

specialised technical knowledge

This is one of the most important steps in generating wealth. This kind of knowledge is the one used to make things, provide services and provide a value. Also, very often, this kind of knowledge is scalable and can bring you a good deal of wealth. Here are some examples that should open your eyes on this very important point:

- What is your practical knowledge when it comes to replacing components in your car?
- Can you fix a broken washing machine? Oven? Microwave? Vacuum cleaner?
- What kind of pump can be used in an ATEX environment?
- How would you speed up an Apache webserver?
- What is the most efficient way to process chipboard?
- What are the things to look after when mixing concrete for a dam?
- What should you look out for when selecting a sterilisation system in a dental practice?
- How do you deal with a broken vertebra?
- Can you write a contract for the merging of two banks?

...and so on.

This is the kind of specialised knowledge you need in order to make money.
For the sake of the argument let's imagine two people living in France: one who specialises in history of medieval Azerbaijan and, another one, who specialises in logistics in the perishable food sector. Which one is going to be exposed to the most opportunities to make money? Who has got a knowledge that can be applied more easily to add value to the consumers?

Remember that:

$$\text{Luck} = \text{Preparation} \times \text{Opportunity}$$

If you're preparing well but the field you've chosen has very few or even no opportunities to make money, then your preparation will not be likely to lead to luck, at least in financial terms. As with everything, there will be exceptions: the historian with a deep knowledge of medieval Azerbaijan and a passion for antiques and travelling, might start a successful chain trading antiques from the region, offering guided tours, and so on.

All our examples are just to transmit an idea, a concept, rather than to specify which sector or which industry is the one that will make you money since, at the end of the day, it's your life we're talking about.

Continuous improvement: general knowledge

In my specific industry, sometimes, you come across people who are so specialised, have a great deal of technical knowledge, really know what they're talking about in technical terms, and that's pretty much it with them. They are great engineers, technicians, accountants, lawyers, manufacturers, and that's where their persona stops, there's nothing more about them. Obviously, no human is devoid of general curiosity but, some people get so taken in by their jobs, their passions, their ideas that they forget that there's more to life than programming, material science, washing machine engineering or derivatives.

Also, if you only possess technical knowledge (or specific knowledge for your service), you might make a lot of money, but you also might lose it as quickly as you gained it. For example, if you're completely oblivious of world politics, of cultures, of history, you're basically like a very skilled sailor who can't see much further into the distance, therefore you may be in the process of very skilfully navigating your ship towards the storm that will sink it.

I've had the displeasure to observe a great company with amazing products, inherited by an oblivious second generation, slowly but steadily dismantled and sabotaged by sheer ignorance. Another company, with great technical skills and products, but a lack of understanding of human nature. But also, how many businesspeople have been caught by the ups and down of history? How many times fortunes have been made thanks to the ability to predict history?

So, while technical knowledge is paramount, you also need general knowledge to capitalise on it, grow your wealth, and not lose everything.

For example, what would happen if you didn't follow the news about politics, you invested a lot of money in properties, and then the government passed a law to make it very expensive to be a landlord? What if you specialise in a sector that then gets overtaken by another emerging one? What if you go on blindly building your business when, the whole area you are serving, goes into long-term decay? Keep your antenna up!

Time management, continuous learning, online courses

If you do a little bit of research you will find that many top investors and business-people read a lot, learn continuously, follow new courses, and are actively looking for information. Lately, I've had some very good ideas about potential products for my company and these ideas all came from a paragraph in an article published by the MIT SLOAN.

In this article the author gave an extremely powerful idea: **nowadays (2020), big profits can be made by making accessible to everybody technologies and products that before were either too difficult to use, too expensive, or not practical to the standard consumer.**

!!! WOW !!!

Have you ever sat down and written a list of business ideas? Have you ever discussed with friends what could be the next big thing? And then nothing really comes to mind.

Exercise – Brainstorming

Now, for the sake of it, try to take in this idea and apply it to something that you know well and like. Is there a technology or a service in your sector that at the moment is limited to the specific industry and specialists, but could be brought to the mass market? Is there a product or service you would want but isn't accessible because of the price, or the required knowledge, and so on?

In this idea there are numerous gold mines for those who are ready to see them.

Finally, it's no news that in the age of constant and instant messaging, online courses, continuous learning, we're always trying to learn something new and always getting distracted, so finding ways to cope with that can be very helpful.

The way I found useful is to do the things at the right time: eating frogs in the morning, doing physical activity at the end of the day, not forcing myself to do something when I really see that I'm wasting time, and trying to do things in blocks of time. There's nothing really new to add here.

Your Connections

I left this point until last and it has not been part of the main strategy because it can be the most complicated of all for the majority of people, and we don't want to build a strategy based on things which are not under our control.

As humans we do not live in a vacuum, but we live in the human society where

we're surrounded by people (and without people around there would be no point in living). In your business, in your job, and in your personal life, you will have people around: friends, relatives, partners, general acquaintances, customers, suppliers, and so forth.
Most of us go through the education system and that's where we meet most people: classmates, people on our basketball team, people in the same club, and so on. The more structured a society is, the more likely it is that the majority of people you know are from institutions, schools, sport avenues, workplaces, and so on. In certain places, indeed, to talk with a stranger on the bus, is perceived as an odd thing to do. Less structured societies can be more open-minded when it comes to connections and probably this attitude provides more social mobility.

As someone who has moved from one country to another and that in and out of eight different houses within less than ten years in the UK, I have had a lot of time to think about this.

When you stick in your hometown or in a university town where there are some good opportunities to pursue a career, you are likely to have a circle of friends and people around you. If, for example, you go to a well-known university in a major city where there are many job opportunities, it's likely that, soon after leaving university, you will be absorbed into the productive tissue of the city and that the same will happen to the people you know.

This in turn means that people who have done similar studies, will be able to keep meeting for coffees, go on holidays together, party and have nights out creating bonds that go beyond the professional sphere and turn into real friendships. This is another kind of 'Eton Effect' where highly educated people go to a good college, then continue to Oxford and Cambridge, and end up in government and the major institutions of the country. Obviously, you don't need to go to Eton to see this, be it Peking University, Harvard, MIT, ETH in Zurich and so on, this effect is well-studied and known.

If you're reading this book, I recognise that it's unlikely you have been to one of those universities, for the simple fact that many people who end up there are either well-supported financially by families who have mastered the art of making money OR are so clever in their specific field that possibly they will not have to struggle with saving money and investing properly but will end up in high-paying jobs that pay six-figure salaries within a few years of graduating.

So, if like me you are 'out of the club', where does this leave you? The answer, as always, is: it leaves you with a lot of work to do.

First of all, as you will learn in the rest of the book, almost everything can be learnt: actors learn to fake accents and roles, people learn foreign languages, table manners, style, art, literature, basically almost everything can be learnt.

If you focus your mind on it, you really can do anything, it's just a matter of the price you're ready to pay in terms of time.

The process is simple:

- Decide your objective
- Establish the price to pay in terms of time
- Pay the price – and often overpay
- Get to the target
- Move on

This means that, it doesn't matter where you come from, what your background is, your starting education level, your financial situation and so on, you can do almost anything, turn into almost anything, and become (or fake it until you become) almost anything if you pay the price in time and effort.

As an Italian living in the UK, I find it quite interesting how many British people have interiorised their belonging to a certain class that they assume the situation cannot change. So much talent is wasted due to self-prejudice.

What does this mean in practical terms?

Let's assume that, for your business to thrive, you need to get some good public contracts from the government. As your business exists now, it can turnover a few tens of thousands of pounds per year, however, if you win the public contract, you can get hundreds of thousands of pounds per year in turnover and make a healthy profit.

Obviously, your company has got the best product or service and you really have a solution or service that can help the government. At this point there are mainly two possibilities:

- The government has a perfectly neutral selection process which means that, it doesn't matter what connections you have with the department, the choice will be purely based on objective criteria
  OR
- The government, despite its best efforts, has not been able to create a process where decisions are taken 100% objectively so the personal element can sway the decision towards you or your competitor.

Before proceeding let me be clear that I'm not talking about corruption or any illegal practices here. What I'm referring to is the simple fact that, despite the best efforts of the system, people like to buy from people that are like them and this means a lot.

Let's assume that the buyer who is responsible for 'objectively' deciding which supplier to use has two choices which are very similar in price and specifications (you and a competitor). Also, let's assume that, during the discussions with you, the way you talked, the things you said and the way you wrote were very different from what the buyer would have done.

On the other hand, the other supplier, was more in tune with the buyer, used the same language, similar style, and incidentally, were part of the same industrial interest group. At the end of the selection process, the buyer decides to buy from the supplier who he feels 'closer' to and for whom he has got some personal references from the interest group they're both members of.

Is this unfair? Is this corruption? Is this elitism? Probably this is simply a reinforcement that:

$$Luck = Preparation \times Opportunity$$

The other supplier, by joining an interest group and creating relationships within that group, was able to establish themselves as the go-to person for that specific product or service. When they joined that interest group years ago, they didn't know that, five years later, there was going to be a public tender for their specific product, but they were simply interested in the subject and decided to join this group to keep abreast of all the latest innovations in the sector.

On the other hand, you were focused exclusively on making a perfect business and shunned those mundane events with no real meaning and, when you needed a reference, you could only give references from customers who were alien to the buyer and from a different sector.

We all lead busy lives, above all if you're still working full-time, trying to pay bills and mortgages, as well as building your own business. However, we have to recognise that interest groups, professional associations, universities, institutions and so on, are places where many of the best minds gather, where new ideas are conceived, where development plans are discussed, and so forth.

As a businessperson, can you afford not to know the names of the owners of the biggest companies in your sector? Can you afford not to know how the people in that sector work/talk/think? The answer is another big fat NO.

So, let's say that you didn't go to a famous college or university but that, given the industry you're in, some 'connections' would be helpful. What should you do? There are many things you might want to consider:

- Going to a university part-time where you can gain some good skills and good connections at the same time

- Find an interest group, a club that you could join
- Find out where the main people you're interested in doing business with spend their time and simply go there and enjoy your time
- Organise some events (conferences, meetings) on a specific topic
- Join some events
- Work towards publications to get your name known

What I'm saying is that, in many industries, you really need to **LIVE and BREATHE the industry** if you want to excel. It can't just be a past-time, something done *en passant*. You have to become one of the pillars, one of the known experts, one of the recognised names in the industry/sector/business.

Now, this advice is more relevant for certain industries compared with others so, for example, if you're a manufacturer of components used in the 5G networks, you'll really need to grow your network and your connections; if you're in the properties business, you'll need to meet estate agents, get a good knowledge of the local property scene, and so on.

On the other hand, if your goods are sold directly to customers (cakes, skates, plants, pots etc.) then you may not need connections in the industry as much, however, being surrounded by like-minded people will always help to generate more ideas, more innovation and more value, and you would still have to develop your personal brand.

Final thoughts on The Junction

We're at the end of this chapter which, probably, is the most important of the whole book. The chapters before this are quite mechanical, in the sense that as long as you implement the strategy and aren't too unlucky, you can expect a certain level of success and income. The chapters after this are more practical with focus on business matters, sales, property management, wealth management, but also more speculative, since the more we move forward in this journey, the more abstract it will be.

Getting to the junction requires a lot of hard work, but almost everybody can do it if they persevere. **What you do AT THE JUNCTION**, however, decides if your strategy will be successful or not, if you'll actually get to the point where you can stop working (if you wanted), or where you make a lot of money (if you want that much), or where you can greatly improve as a person (if that's your aspiration).

We've seen that with properties and business, you'll have to make judgement calls based on your actual circumstances, on the market, and on the economic situation in general. With yourself, you should not make compromises and try to improve your skills, knowledge and understanding of the world, if not for making money then just to be a better human.

Finally, don't forget that people buy from people and that the people who surround you will shape your thoughts, your ideas, and can give you some great input, so try to grow your connections accordingly, not simply because of the benefit, but and mainly because, people who are pushing the boundaries, that are working hard, that want to make things happen, fellow entrepreneurs and high achievers, specialist and technicians, politicians and VIPs tend to be interesting people to spend time with.

The Italian general manager (now deceased) of Fiat Chrysler Automobiles, Sergio Marchionne, used to welcome employees with this letter:

Dear Colleague

There is a world where people do not let things happen. They make them happen. They do not forget their dreams in the drawer, they hold them tightly in their hands. They throw themselves into the fray, savour the risk, leave their mark. It is a world in which every new day and every new challenge gives the opportunity to create a better future. Who lives in that place, never lives the same day twice, because he knows that it is always possible to improve something.

People, there, feel they belong to that exceptional world as much as it belongs to them. They bring it to life with their work, they model it with their talent. Their values are impressed in an indelible way. Maybe it will not be a perfect world and it's certainly not easy. No one is sitting on the side lines and the pace can be frenetic, because these people are passionate — intensely passionate — at what they do. Those who choose to live there because they believe that taking responsibility gives a deeper meaning to their work and life.

Welcome to that world

***

Now, as a creator of wealth, it is your choice to join that world or even better create your own version of it.

Up to this point in the book I have shared mainly information and knowledge that I have personally applied in its entirety to start and grow my own business, create a modest property portfolio, and gain specialised knowledge and good connections in my specific field.

We've seen how, starting from 'zero', it's possible to build a decent base from which you can aspire to even more wealth, independence, and freedom. In the coming chapters I will continue sharing even more applied knowledge that has allowed businesses I have been directly involved with to grow in the last ten years (2010-2020), and that has been beneficial in the management of my rental income.

At this point in the book I'll assume that you've taken certain decisions when at The Junction, so you are now well-versed in the management of your finances, have a solid financial position, own at least three or four properties with attached mortgages, have a business that has been running for some time, are continuing to study and specialise, and might have even kept your job to maximise your income and saving power.

Moreover, you have decided that you will continue pushing because you want to have a sustainable business, an established property portfolio, and a greater level of freedom.

Finally, since this is likely something that you're reading all in one go, after purchasing this book, my strong suggestion is to keep this book with you and implement and review the different ideas as your plan progresses. It's also likely that some of the names, tools and practices I mention in 2020, won't be 100% valid in 2030, so you will have to adapt that to your present situation.

NOTICE: EVERYTHING TO THIS POINT IS PERFECTLY FEASIBLE

IF YOU WANT MONEY, NOW YOU CANNOT SAY
"I DON'T KNOW WHERE TO START"
WE JUST SPENT DOZENS OF PAGES DESCRIBING ALL THE PRACTICAL ACTIONS
YOU NEED TO TAKE

Chapter 10 – Your real business

This chapter is all about the practical aspects of business, no nonsense, no motivational speeches. We will restart from where we left off, which is you running your business alongside your main job, and reach the point where you'll be working full-time on your business (if you decide to do so). This chapter, for its very nature is quite long compared with the others so it might make sense to break it into pieces when you read it.

Your job and your business

The first questions you might have is: "I've read up to this point, but I'm not yet sure on how I can work on my business if most of my day is taken by my main job... also, what if they find out? Will I lose my job/?". Let's clear these doubts once and for all.

<u>Your business name and address: Tax-Free, Sole Trader</u>

This example is specific to the UK and it may differ in other countries, however, some of the expedients can be used and, as always, it's more about the mindset than about the specific points.

We saw that you don't need to register a limited company, but you can simply trade tax-free up to £1,000 and then as a sole trader above £1,000. When you're trading tax-free, realistically speaking, you haven't set up a website and have probably landed a few jobs/orders (depending on what you do) by word of mouth or trusted contacts, you might want to make a page on social media or any other informal means and probably, the only ones who will find out who you are, are your customers and people you choose to target for advertisement. At this stage, it's very easy to conceal/manage your activity.

As things grow past £1,000, you now need to operate as a sole trader and here you have to use your name, but you might want to use a 'Trading Name', for example, 'The Futuristic Accountant' or 'Industrial Parts Factory Wales', and in that case on your legal paperwork you should add this sentence: 'John Smith trading as The Futuristic Accountant'.

For many people who are scared "to be found out" by their current employer, the idea of putting their name on official paperwork, websites and so on, is scary for the simple reason of: "what if someone at the office googles my name? My home address?", which is fully understandable. For what concerns the address, if you need to put one, you could use the address of your rental property which is probably not easily linkable to yourself. For your name these are the solutions:

Solution 1 – The incomplete website

If someone is ever going to find out about your activity outside work, this will be via a website. However, if the nature of your own business means that you can start doing some business without a fully published website then, while you're still testing the water, you might decide to:

- Buy a domain name anyway to give your email address some credibility
- Put a page with a basic description and the infamous "coming soon…." (not ideal but it might be necessary)
- Approach your customers directly using email, phone, social media
- Put the full 'John Smith trading as The Futuristic Accountant' only where strictly necessary (legal docs, invoices etc.)

The advantage of this approach is that it's coherent with the stage at which your company is: the very beginning. Also, it gives you perfect control of who you contact, and it creates no hassle.

Solution 2 – A website with exclusions

Depending on your contract, your risk aversion, and other variables, you might decide to press on and get a fully working website and implement a full marketing approach. In this case, on your website you will need to explicitly say 'John Smith trading as The Futuristic Accountant', however, you might want to say that ONLY on specific pages, such as terms and conditions, company information, privacy and contact page.

There's a little trick that can help you here: robots.txt and the noindex directive. Again, this can seem too technical but again, making money and managing money is about technicalities, get used to it. By putting a .txt file in your website root folder and a noindex directive in these pages, you can tell Google which pages you DO NOT want Google to index. So, you might have a perfectly optimised website for your roofing business or for your accounting business in the local area and still make it difficult for someone to find it out by simply checking your name on the internet.

This method is not bullet-proof, but it allows you to still be coherent and credible, while somehow concealing your identity.

Solution 3 – Your partner

A third solution, depending on the line of work and business, could be to involve your partner or relatives and use their name in this initial phase when you're testing the water: they will be the sole trader. You need to check this practice is OK in your country, but there should be no problem as long as there's coherence. In this case, you would be working for free and the profits will go to your partner/brother/sister who will then do the self-assessment, but you would get the benefit of testing the market and potentially starting to establish a name/brand.

Certainly, this can be quite risky since, as a sole trader, your partner will be liable with all their assets if someone decides to sue you (them) and, while you might be willing to take that risk for yourself, you should be very clear about the liabilities when involving others.

Also, this is a temporary solution and, as soon as you see it working you should then go back to Solution 1 or 2 or, even better, register a limited company.

<u>Your business name and address: a limited company</u>

The beauty of a limited company is that it's something completely separated from you, what belongs to the company does not belong directly to you, the name of the company can't be directly associated with you, and the address of the company doesn't have to be your home address.

This also offers a greater level of protection: if you make a big business mistake and another company or individual sues your company for damages, your responsibility is limited to how much you can actually afford in the company: they can't come after your assets or your money, and basically you're even more protected from bankruptcy[15]. You can close the company and the debts end with the company, as long as haven't done anything illegal.

For what concerns the address, this can be your accountant's address, which will usually offer the service for a fee.

For what concerns the company shareholder (which is usually information reported on governmental websites which are then indexed by Google), depending on the level of paranoia and trust, you might decide to make your partner the only shareholder and, at the same time, sign an agreement without a date for the transfer of the shares.

In this way, the owner of the company is your partner or relative until you put a date on the agreement and the shares and ownership are passed to you. By doing this you can build a whole business and test the idea without anybody from your main job ever knowing about it. This also means that should your partner or relative change their mind, you could have some big issues and that, until the company reaches a certain point and you're ready to jump, you won't be able to pay yourself a salary unless you become an employee of the company. That, however, might have some tax implications which will be reflected on your tax code that your em-

---

[15] As long as there's no criminal offence, or you did it on purpose.

ployer might then notice.

Finally, you might want to use an alias, an abbreviation, or even a fake name (or better your partner/director name) for emails if you're really that worried.

Noncompeting clause

It goes without saying that, if in your contract of employment there are non-competing clauses, you should really pay attention that you do not compete. If you start stealing customers and business from your main employer, you might be in big trouble. Moreover, this is deeply unethical since your employer is a businessperson who has their own struggles so, as long as your **side business does not interfere with their business,** it's fine. When it starts to affect it, you should consider your position.

Managing time and location

So now that we have covered the practical aspects of starting the side business and minimising the risk of being "found out", let's see how you can manage time.

Ideally, as in the case of Xiaohui and Jenny, you're living somewhere near to your workplace. This means you might even walk to your workplace, that you don't need a second car, and that you're saving time and money.

Most of these conditions depend on the commitment to a specific plan, for example, if you know that your final objective is to run your own business in a specific sector and have a number of properties, you could decide to:

- Get a job in that specific sector
- Buy a not-so-expensive house as near as possible to the office to reduce commuting time
- Work hard at your main job so that you can build up your knowledge and network
- Compromise on location and working hours

Laser focus on achieving this is needed, and, possibly, many aspects of your life will have to go in the same direction.

If you're commuting three to four hours per day by car, it's basically impossible to really start your business: if you're driving you should be focused on driving and, the only thing you might be able to do, are phone calls to potential customers, while driving, with an unstable line and fighting with the traffic – the perfect recipe for disaster, stress and low productivity.

Also, at the weekends you're likely to be very tired, and if you're doing only one day of work per week, it will take you seven times longer to get to a certain point compared with someone who is working full time.

Too long, too inefficient, just don't do it, you will burn out.

If you're commuting by train or public transport, unless you're lucky enough to always have a place to sit down and no changes, using that time to do anything productive is very difficult and tiring. I used to study chemistry on a train when following a course with the Open University, but it was hard work and I wasn't putting too much effort into my main job which I was planning to leave.

So, really, if you're planning to work on your business, you need some things to be in some sort of order first: where you live, how you get to work, how long it takes you to get there, how you're paying the bills and mortgages, and so on. This might mean that you end up in a small city in a boring place, or that you're next to an industrial estate with nothing exciting about it, but, if your commute is fifteen minutes to work rather than sixty, you're saving one and a half hours per day, which is almost eight hours per week, and you will still have energy at night and during the weekends.

All of a sudden, you have eight to twelve hours on a Saturday, the same on a Sunday, three or four hours on weekdays, and you're now almost competing at the same level as someone who's working full-time at their own business, without the extra stress and with no need to pillage your own company of profits that you can instead reinvest into the company itself to grow it quicker.

A sample schedule could be something like:

6:00 – 6:30: Wake up, breakfast, shower
6:30 – 8:30: Work on your own business
8:30 – 9:00: Commute, get to the office in advance
9:00 - 13:00: Work at your main job
13:00 – 14:00: Lunch plus time for a couple of phone calls
14:00 – 17:00: Work at your main job
17:00 – 17:30: Commute back home, shopping on the way
17:30 – 21:30: Work on your company and have a light dinner
21:30 – 22:30: Don't fool yourself, your brain ain't working anymore – time for exercise, yoga, running
Saturday/Sundays/Days off: this is when you get most things done.

Now **this is more of an ambition than a specific schedule to respect**. Depending on your other commitments, you may need more or less time for certain things, however two elements are clear:
- You need to be in a good location or arrangement with your main job
- You need to sacrifice your time

As always, **this is the slow and effective way!**

Managing calls, emails and urgent requirements

Some of you may be thinking: "The nature of my sector means that I really need to answer the phone when someone calls" or "I can't take calls".

Another piece of good news: virtual assistants/secretaries. There are services that, for a standard standing charge plus a charge per minute, can have a very professional sounding secretary taking messages for you. A professional secretary will answer the phone for you at a specified number, say something: "Such and Such Associates, how may I help?", take the message, contact details and names and then send you an email. You can then follow up at lunchtime or later in the evening.

Another option is to have two mobile phones since you can simply get the missed calls and then call the potential customers back when you can.

Synergies

When your business and your main line of work are in the same business, there are some great things that can happen. You will start to see that, the work you carry out for your own business will help your boss' businesses and vice versa. This is another reason to keep your job and your company as long as possible: people you will meet through your main job, might, one day, become your customers for a non-competing product or service, they might become the specialists you rely on to make your business prosper, your mentors and your friends.

My strong suggestion is that you shouldn't shy away from work on your main job and also share the knowledge, the skills, and anything else that can be useful from one place to the other.

Once I found myself spending two months doing a list of potential customers at my main job, before I even started to work on my own business, and then, months later, I was able to recycle that list for my own business: I just saved two months and generated some business.

Your own office

Before you jump and check on Google what's the best available price for office space, remember that the best way to make money is not to spend it in the first place. So, unless it's really necessary, at the beginning, and for as long as it is reasonable, your home will also be your office.

Ideally, you want a separate room to avoid distractions, if it's not possible then a corner with a proper office desk and chair, a second screen and good lighting is important. This is all assuming that you don't need a workshop (which might be a shed in your garden) or a room (which might be your sacrificed living room).

Your product/service

Now that we've cleared once and for all the practicalities of working on two things at the same time, let's look at the product or service you are offering. I will only refer to product for simplicity from now on.

Exercise – Basics

Do you know your product well? Is it something you have had direct experience of in a commercial/industrial environment for a few months/years? Do you really understand the product, the value it adds, why people buy it, what benefit it brings, the competition, how you can be different, and so on? Try to answer these simple questions:

- Have you researched your own product well enough? I'm not talking about being able to explain the product to a standard customer, but I'm talking about being able to talk with an expert without seeming clueless.
- Do you know why customers buy it? What is the benefit they're looking for?
- Do you know how it works in depth?
- Will you be able to offer support and guidance to customers?
- Have you researched the competition? This is the big one! People say they've researched the competition when what they actually mean is that they can somehow mis-spell their competitors name and have a vague feeling about what their competitors do. This is not enough, you really should know your competitors' products, offers, prices, way of selling, so that, once a potential customer comes to you after having talked with another three competitors, you really do know where you stand.

The important point here is that you should be able to talk about what you're offering and should be knowledgeable on the subject. There's no point starting a business or registering a limited company if you have still that much to learn. Once you're some sort of 'expert' and know enough to explain costs, benefits, functionalities, features, comparisons with the competition, you can move to the next step.

Exercise – Intermediate

Now that you have a vague idea of what you're doing, the next questions you should ask yourself are:

- How can I source this product? Where can I buy it from in bulk?
- How can I make it? Where can I buy the ingredients/components?

- What are the physical processes involved from start (production/sourcing) to finish (delivery/use/installation)?
- What are the costs associated with all of this? How can I minimise them? Is there any way to reduce the costs?
- Do I need any special permit? License? Certificate?
- What are the practical steps?
  Make a diagram on a piece of paper of how you see the process working and look for things that you are missing, that could go wrong and how to rectify them.
- Have you codified these steps in formal documents?

Start implementing all of the above and learn as you go along.

Exercise – Advanced

Despite your best efforts, you've still only got a vague idea of how your product really works and you still have a general understanding of the technicalities of it and the market in general.

For example, you may be selling soap and you may be using a special machine to make it, but you're still struggling to understand how it works. You may be producing food products and you understand how to make great sauces, however you're still missing the secret ingredient and you feel there's still space for improvement in your process and so on.

At this point you might want to consider:

- What's the established competition doing and how can you do it better, cheaper or in a personalised way?
- Can you easily branch out to serve new markets?
- Are there any other markets that you could serve?
- Have you matched your competitors for price and quality, if not, why not?
- What can you do about it?

Only once you have **somehow matched some of the established competitors** and have developed a brand, you can think about how to go on and improve. You might use personalisation of your product to develop a USP, but you should also aim to imitate the quality of the top competitors.

Going through that process will help you and your business to gain experience through marginal increments and also push your processes towards better and better standards.

How do you get your customers?

As you're working on your product idea, you really need to focus on how to attract customers: this is called customers acquisition. You might be in a position where you're getting customers by word of mouth, from the internet, from social media, from local advertisement or they're just walking into your shop. It might be that you're already quite busy, but **you have not thought about how you actually find customers** and this is the time to do it, before you run out of customers, money or luck.

As for everything, if you Google 'how to get more customers' and 'customer acquisition', you'll find all the knowledge of the world, the problem is that you won't read it, probably because most of it is trying to sell you a special course, a subscription to a newsletter to then drip-feed you news until you buy an ultimate guide, or simply… because it's too "complex".

When I studied marketing during a sort of MBA, we learnt so much on how to use advanced marketing techniques that, in the real world, you don't have the cash nor the capabilities to deploy, so they're basically useless.

Here's a practical list of things you can do to get customers in 2020s (not in order of importance) but, before doing that, let's clear an important point:

To find OR to be found…this is the question.

Everybody who has worked in sales knows the word 'target' and 'forecast', everybody has been told to call more customers and has been asked where the next new project is going to come from.

There's one fundamental truth and I want you to think deeply about this:

- When was the last time you were sold something you didn't want to buy?
- When was the last time you answered an unknown number and handed out your bank details?
- When was the last time someone emailed you out of the blue and you thought "this is great, I'm buying it!"

I can't remember any time in the last ten years when this has happened, and those poor souls really tried hard.

The truth is that, more and more, customers (us) like to choose, to get informed, evaluate and eventually buy something that we want, need and can afford.

One summer, the weather was extremely hot outside and the cellar which I used as my studio was getting very humid and unusable. There's no other place in the house that I could easily use as a studio with my PC, two screens etc. and also, moving the whole thing, was very unpractical. After some searches on the internet on basement ventilation, humidity, heat transfer and so on, I got a rough idea of what I needed: a dehumidifier, around £100, for a small room and a supplier with many good reviews. The studio was used only for my business in those days which meant that the dehumidifier was a business expense. So, after going on the internet and looking for some models, I bought one using my company card, saving 20% of VAT which I got back later on.

This process is repeated millions of times across the world, day in and day out: people feel a need, look for answers, get some information, decide and buy. For this reason, I strongly believe that:

The real battle in 2020s is the one to be found.

The last twenty or thirty years really mean that 'Sales and Marketing', in many markets has become 'Marketing and Sales', where the marketing is the necessary first step.

Imagine you walk into a town centre full of shops, some are small, some are big. Many hustlers on the street try to convince you to get into a specific shop but then, there's one which is amazing, big, well-presented, with a huge variety of products and services. Which one do you see first? Which shop is more likely to attract the most people? We know the answer.

Obviously, if you enter into this perfect shop and nobody welcomes you and asks you the right questions to help you choose, you might just go inside, have a look and move on, so that's where the sales are important, however, you need to be found in the first place.

This means that, most of the time, it's better to be found by the customers than to 'hunt' for customers, people don't want to be hunted down and stripped of all their money. On the contrary, people want to find what they want and need and then be enabled and reassured that their decision is the right one.

For this reason, we'll focus first on how to get found and then on how to actively find customers.

Be found by your customers.

Exercise – LinkedIn

Depending on your situation you might want to:
- Update your personal profile and/or use your partner's profile (if possible)

- Make a company page, especially if you're in the industrial market and you deal with suppliers from overseas
- Try LinkedIn Ads where you can target extremely specific groups of people by selecting age, region, job titles and so on.

I find this extremely useful for those companies that work in the field of Business to Business (B2B) sales because you can show your advert directly on the timeline of specific people. Also, your LinkedIn profile and network are, in very brutal terms, free marketing: using LinkedIn to find a job is when you have the employee mindset, using LinkedIn to connect with customers/partners is the entrepreneur's mindset.

Exercise – Google

There are thousands of books and tutorials about Google and Search Engine Optimisation (SEO), here's a very direct list of the steps you need to take to be successful on Google. In this list EVERY word has a meaning, don't just glide over it but implement it all.

- Register your domain, ideally with a local extension: .es, .fr, .co.uk etc.
- Make sure your domain name contains either a keyword or your company name, or both, or register two domains: one for SEO and one for corporate presence. Double work and more effective.
- Use a simple directory structure (domain.com/product-one/ is better than domain.com/cms/en/products/sub-products/product-one/)
- Make sure your website has all the relevant content with long pages and:
    - Contains a minimum of 500 words per page, but aim much higher
    - Be interesting and engaging for the reader (it's all nice and good if your customer arrives on your website but not good if they don't get in touch!)
    - Have understandable text, broken into readable paragraphs, with some words in bold (<strong>) in each paragraph
    - Contain images that you have created and that are relevant
    - Contain VIDEOS which are very important
    - Use valid code (W3C standard), good page speed, good accessibility, fully responsive
    - Ideally have a comment section
    - Be always updated with new and relevant content, videos and so on

As you're working on your business website, you also want to take the following steps:

- Register and optimise on Google My Business
- Register all the other social media profiles

- Install Google Analytics and use it, use it and use it to get the most out of it
- Register and study Google Search Console – extremely important
- If needed/helpful also start a Google Website for your business

SEO: Search Engine Optimisation

For this my only advice is **learn from the best**.

There are millions of people saying that they know SEO, that they can teach you how to be the best on Google, that they can bring you to the first page in six months for a very competitive keyword or that they are Google Certified. After some careful investigation, most of these companies are either:

- Desperately trying to play the numbers' game in an over-saturated market
- Really serious and charge a fortune which you probably can't invest at this point

So, if you're a business owner, just go on Google and search for 'SEO 2020'. Whoever has written something which is on the first result of Google for SEO 2020 knows what they are talking about. In my case, I go to this page: https://backlinko.com/seo-this-year which is incidentally from the website I followed to get on the top of Google for most of the keywords I'm interested in with my business.

As you'll see, again, this is a lot of hard work.

Location and the look of your shop

It goes without saying that if you have a shop, the location is paramount and you'll have to find the perfect mix between rental price, footfall, demographics, potential growth, kind of customers and other similar factors. Also, the way your shop looks is extremely important: do you give a professional feeling, or does it look run down? This can make the world of difference.

Find your customers

While it's important to be found by customers, if there are two companies, A and B, where A is only perfecting the art of 'be found' marketing and B is perfecting both 'find' and 'be found', who has more chances to get customers? The answer is B, it's as simple as that and it's a numbers' game.

Also, in certain industries customers EXPECT to be found: why should I look for something if three salespeople are going to call me anyway in the coming week? One of them has also delivered a good pitch and it sounded convincing.

Prospection lists

If you're in the B2B sector, there are good chances that you can create a list of potential customers by searching for specific keywords on Google. Then you use the list you've generated to carry out the following activities. A list for prospection could look something like this:

Customer	Website	Main Phone	Contact Person	Contacted	Notes
Company	www.som...com	+44 7675...	Jonny	10/10/2020	Recall in 3 weeks

There are also other sources where you can buy lists of data (from data brokers, electoral registry and so on).

Cold and warm calling

This is the most dreaded one, very few people like it because, simply put, very few people like to be rejected hundreds of times per day, it really takes motivation and thick skin. At this point just remember that: SW SW SW SW

Some will
Some won't
So what?
So, who's next?

Cold and warm emailing

In the EU, with the new GDPR regulations, you can't just spam everybody with an email: it's illegal and also a waste of time. What you can do however, is send specific emails to specific people in an organisation. Do your research, find out who the relevant people are, and connect with them.

Messaging on LinkedIn and other professional networks

This is also a good way. Usually, the best introductions are those that point to a general reason why the person should connect with you such as "we're in the same sector and we might share opportunities and information".

Leaflets, traditional mailing

If your business is very local, posting leaflets and similar activities can be useful.

Be among your customers

There is a third way which doesn't involve being found or finding customers which is: to be among them. This is what's called networking or having connections and usually can be in very different forms such as: conferences, exhibitions, academia and interest groups.

Some final thoughts on how you get your customers

It's paramount that you have, in your mind, on paper, on an Excel spreadsheet, a formalised way on how you get your customers: a simple strategy, a list of actions, of advertisement platforms, of numbers to call. You need to have a clear focus on what and how you get your customers.

You also want to get a good feeling of what works and what doesn't work. You might find that for your particular business you need to make a hundred phone calls a day prospecting for customers (I used to do that for one of my businesses) and, on another one, two significant calls per week are enough. In any case, you need a codified way, a *modus operandi*, a consistent set of actions that work for your business and bring more customers.

Once you find what works (cold calling, leaflets, online ads), just do more of it and leave what doesn't work, so experimentation is the key here. If your budget is £300 for advertising, then spend £60 on LinkedIn ads, £40 on Google PPC, £60 on leafletting, £100 on cold calling and canvassing and then decide which one works for you.

Data and Systems

Years ago, I had one thought: "If I had a magic button that I could press to get:

- a website done in such and such way
- technical knowledge
- a list of five thousand people from my industry to write to
- agreements with Supplier A, B and C
- a good understanding of my obligations as a limited company
- all the company stationery, marketing, brochures etc. done professionally
- a CRM system with such and such options
- a home office and workshop space
- all the manuals and materials translated into the target language

then, I would push this button and get all of this done and I would already have a good business in place making a few thousand pounds of profit every month".

But this magic button doesn't exist, so unfortunately there's no magic button to press.

However, this thought just **made me realise an amazing truth**: there is no magic in business, nothing mysterious or esoteric, no secret mindset that's only accessible to the few. There's only one harsh reality: who can do the best job, in the quickest way, at the best price, and optimise their efforts.

Imagine this magic button as your time. To do all the things above it can take ten years, five years or less than one year and much of it depends on:

- how long you work and how focused you are
- how many consistent and clever decisions you make
- how many times you remake the same thing
- how ready you are to undertake a lot of hard work at the beginning

If you have a very good execution of all I have mentioned above, you will do well eventually. If you make mistakes, you slow down and possibly fail.

Some examples

You could work extremely hard but make a lot of mistakes, poor strategic decisions, wrong calls, lack the skills to actually do things, and eventually end up 'wasting' all that effort.

You could also make brochures once, by yourself, to save some money, then do them again, and again, and again and try five or ten different versions of your logo and your whole marketing strategy; you would eventually get there but wouldn't it be better to just pay a professional, get those templates done once and for all, and use them for five years rather than five weeks?

At the same time, you might spend too much money on marketing and run out of cash and eventually close your business.

You might not have a proper CRM system because you think you can use Excel. Time goes on, the business grows, and three years later you've lost track and have to spend months inputting old data that you could have been inputted in a database since the beginning.

You might decide that some legal documents, such as terms and conditions of sale, can be postponed, until you then have to quote for a big project and you need it, so then you rush through it and hope for the best.

You might think that accounting is boring, leave it until the last minute and then have to spend hours to find an invoice for some stationery that you bought and so on.

A system made up of systems

Your business is a system used to add value through work and applied knowledge and it is made up of different systems. It's like an engine: the better oiled and designed it is, the less friction there is, the smoother the operation, the quicker it can go. On the other hand, if it isn't well-designed, the oil is old and viscous, and the operation is cranky, it won't go far, might stop or might even explode.

Let's look now at some of these systems.

Exercise - The sales and marketing system

We've already discussed this extensively in the previous pages, so what I want you to do is to focus on the system aspect. Here's a list of things to consider:

- Have you got a marketing plan, a calendar where you note which activities are going to be carried out and when?
- Is there a recurring publishing system such as: a newsletter every month, an article every two months, a blog post every week? Are you trying to implement it as much as possible?
- Is there a sales activity plan such as: twenty prospecting phone calls per day, leaflet drop-off every four weeks, email database every three months, fifteen connections via LinkedIn per day?
- If you are cold calling, have you put a script together? Are you recording your phone calls? Have you structured your sales pitch in a good way? Carried out research on that?
- In your calendar, have you allowed for experimentation? For randomness?
- Have you put in place a document control system? Do you know where all your brochures are? All your legal documents? How many pages has your website got? When were they last updated?

Marketing and sales calendar

This is very similar to my own marketing calendar. As you will see, this focuses more on the B2B sector rather than B2C (Business to Consumer), but you'll get the idea. I have two calendars: one which is the same for every month and one which is more general and done once per year.

All these are on a spreadsheet called 'Things To Do' and each one is an Excel sheet. In this way, when I wake up in the morning, I can look in one place and know what to do.

Recurring Marketing Calendar

1st
- Review Google Analytics from the previous month
- Identify one page where I'm losing traffic and write down things to improve/test

- Review Google Search Console for issues and problems
- Post content on LinkedIn to sponsor a specific page and add likes and comments on selected groups/topics

2nd – 6th
- Improve marketing material
- Work on article/case study/newsletter

7th
- Social media post on products, plus comments and likes
- Send newsletter out to existing contacts
- Publish simple case study for product application

8th – 13th
- Work on content for new product line
- Go through the contacts and send a personalised message

14th
- Social media post on products, plus comments and likes
- Publish a new in-depth article on the website on the 'Topic of the Month'
- LinkedIn campaign update with new product/focus
- Post on Google Business

15th – 20th
- More improvement of existing material
- Make one video on a product
- Get one backlink from a relevant website

21st
- Social media post on products, plus comments and likes
- Google PPC review for specific product

22nd – 27th
- Time to catch up

28th
- Social media post on products, plus comments and likes
- Publish post related to my sector but with no commercial value

Recurring Sales Calendar (assuming you're working at your main job too)

1st, 10th and 20th of the month
- Review all projects, get in touch with all the partners, follow up projects/sales that should happen shortly or might need an extra push

Every day – When you're working:
6:30 – 8:30
- Make a list of potential customers
- Start calling them between 8:00 and 8:30, ideally get around five email addresses

13:00 – 14:00
- More phone calls at lunchtime

17:30 – bedtime
- Here you send all the emails to people/businesses who were interested
- And make more lists of people to call

Every day – When you have taken days off to work on your business:
8:00 – 17:00:
- Phone calls to all the numbers and businesses you have ALREADY organised in a list
- Discussions with potential/existing customers

17:00 – 22:00
- Organise your project lists and CRM
- Keep everything in order
- Eat and sleep

Yearly marketing and sales calendar (for year one of your business)

January
- Register website, social media and all the relevant accounts
- Link posting using IFTTT
- Have all the text content for the website ready and professionally copywritten/proofread
- Commission a graphic designer to help with the logo, look, colour scheme, business cards, brochures and general identity of the business
- Commission a web designer on Fiverr or another freelancing site to come up with a template following the guidelines of the graphic designer

February
- Get website published with all texts and brochures complete
- Update all social media accounts accordingly
- Now the website is ready to go (assuming a small website with ten to fifteen pages, otherwise it will take longer)

March
- Launch first marketing campaign via LinkedIn, Google PPC

- Phone two hundred businesses that might be interested in the product to ask where we can send some marketing material to; hopefully get a name and a non-generic email address (first touch)
- Send at least two hundred slightly personalised emails with marketing and propose a meeting (second touch)

April
- Try, as far as possible, to be seen by those businesses: ads on the streets, LinkedIn, Google, specialised review (third touch)
- Call back all those that haven't answered to ask if they've received the marketing material and if it's possible to organise a face-to-face or virtual meeting
- Phone another two hundred new customers, email them etc.

May
- As in April, focus on prospecting
- Test something new!
- Review of results and re-focus priorities if needed

June – August
- Website and marketing revamp to bring it up to the standard of your best competitor
- Get three articles ready and published in relevant magazines or online publications
- SEO implemented at 100%
- Go on with calls and emails
- Review results

September-December
- More of what has worked in the previous months
- Polish it up until you make it gleam

Some final thoughts on these schedules

You make plans so that you can break them, this is really a universal rule in business. So, when you write down your strategy and plan, **do not** spend days making a perfectly timed plan, and also, do not try to predict what will happen: a plan is more like a guideline, it's something that will allow you to know where to focus and what to do when you wake up in the morning. It isn't a Gant chart for the building of a nuclear power plant, it's more of a compass that defines the direction of travel.

So, if after a few months, you're completely drowning in work and at 23:00 you can't be bothered to post an update on your social media profile, or if one day you really want to sleep until 8:00, don't be too harsh with yourself.
Business is more like a marathon than a sprint: if you keep going long enough, your

name will have been seen more times, you will have more customers, you will have better systems and procedures and, eventually, you get to a critical mass of product and service quality, brand awareness, marketing quality and so on, that you make a breakthrough.

So, remember that the important thing is to:

keep going until you reach that critical mass.

Since you're working full-time to keep the cash coming in, even if you have the best possible synergies and procedures and you're a very effective implementer of your own strategies, you will need to:

- Use Saturdays and Sundays mainly for your marketing and production activities
- During the week, use the early morning and your lunch break to keep things moving
- During the week, use the evenings to do more work (sales, marketing, production)
- Use your holidays for your business – not all!

By doing this:

- Every year you've got almost thirty days of full-time work going towards your business from your holidays (usually twenty to thirty days per year in the West)
- Every year you can get one hundred and four days coming from your weekends
- Every year you get another hundred days coming from your work early in the morning, at lunch time and in the evenings

So, in total, with some consistent sacrifice, you can basically run an almost full-time business while also working at a full-time job.

If we put aside the obvious fact that this is tiring, very tiring, to do, this should also show you that it's feasible.

Using this model, you can keep going at your business, without having to worry at all about money coming in, giving time for your business to mature (some business processes cannot be sped up), and giving you time to test and learn without money worries.

Also, this means that, if you ever lose your job, this will come almost as good news: by this time you will be so tired and shattered by this rhythm of working that, once you get made redundant, you'll actually think: "Phew! Finally, I can focus on my own business". The same goes for your partner and other people that you have involved in the business. From this moment on you will actually never have the problem of "not knowing what to do" because the Sales and Marketing calendars will never end. You can *always* do more sales and more marketing!

Document control systems

Another important part of your sales and marketing system is a document control system. This can be something as simple as an Excel spreadsheet or as complicated as a bespoke software. For a start-up business, an Excel spreadsheet is enough. But what does your document control system do?

What you really want is a list of all your marketing documents, with a code, a version, a last modified date, and a way to file older versions. While this can be seen as boring administration, it has three key functions:

- Keep things in order: you can quickly check all your documents and if they need to be updated
- Keep track of things: sometimes when you change a document (i.e. brochure) you also need to change other things and having a list helps a lot
- Keep track of what you said or wrote: if you made a brochure/leaflet offering a special offer/service and then you change it without saving the old copy, how do you know what you promised to your customer?

A simple system could be something like:

Doc. Code	Filename	Location	Version	Last Update	Comments
DOCBR001	Brochure01.doc	/docs/brochures/	1.0	01/01/2020	Specs changing in 2021

Also, adding an issue number, a version and a publication date to your documents will make your company look more professional: if you've bothered to have a DCS it means that your company is a decent one and that you're doing things properly.

The CRM – Customer Relationship Management System

This is the other big one: a CRM or Customer Relationship Management System. These are systems (software) used to keep track of and manage customers.

Depending on your line of work and your business, you might need a CRM straight away or later on but, it doesn't matter what your business is, you need a central database with all your customers and contacts on it.

Unless you sell to ten big customers and never plan to do anything more than that, you'll easily end up with a lot of information such as company websites, contact details, random bits of information about what a person likes, thinks and wants and so on. Trying to keep everything on an Excel spreadsheet is sheer madness and I've seen that approach fail several times.

On the other hand, if you've been in a big and dysfunctional company, you probably know very well that the CRM could become a torture tool for salespeople or a useless show-how-active-I-am tool for employees that want to show off their activity.

Unless there's a specific reason, you don't need to log every call you make, every email you send, every tiny detail. At the same time, I like to keep track of when was the last time I followed up on a project so that I don't leave them for months without any activity.

Some of the most common CRMs include Sales Cloud, SugarCRM and Zoho. Some of them have very advanced features with calendars, email archiving add-ons directly from Outlook, and so on. Years ago, I found a very good, easy to install and easy to use CRM called EspoCRM which I find very good for small and medium businesses. What you probably want in a CRM for your start-up business are some basic functions, such as:

- Creating accounts (other businesses or customers)
- Associate contacts to these accounts
- Be able to attach files to contacts/accounts
- Log opportunities and have some sort of pipeline
- Set reminders and tasks
- Set different users so that you can add salespeople to your company

That's pretty much all you need from a CRM.

One function which I liked in SugarCRM was the ability to archive emails on the database, however, that comes at a cost which you might not be able to afford at the beginning.

Email shots, newsletters

With GDPR these can seem things of the past, however, there are ways to build a GDPR compliant list of people that you can then contact via email shots and/or newsletters.

The first step, as always, is to make a lot of work and generate a content, a service or an approach which makes people want to be in a mailing list. Today, I opened my email and was very happy to see a newsletter from a company in my same sector.

With all the spam that we get every day, how do you think that's possible? Here's how:

- Each newsletter has unique – really unique – content
- Information on different products, always including something very new
- Then there's a very personal story from the owner about some interesting volunteering activities
- And finally, one in-depth article

For me, their newsletter, is a very good way to keep an eye on what's coming to the market and gain some in-depth knowledge. At the same time, this newsletter reminds me of what this business partner can offer and, when I come across a customer who might need some of their products, I always redirect them to this company.

Certainly, that takes a lot of work, so we're always heading towards the same point: there's no magic buttons in business, but a lot of consistent work.

!!! TIME FOR A PAUSE !!!

You bought this book because you wanted money, or at least so you thought. In this book and in this very specific section I'm explaining, to you, in detail, all the actions that you need to take to make money: installing CRMs, calling customers, delivering products, perfecting marketing campaigns, and so on.

As I'm going through these things, your head starts to wander, you start to watch some random videos on YouTube, look out of the window, open the fridge and eat something.

So, here you are, with a book in your hands which is telling you the 3,000 steps that can help you make £300,000 for sure in less than seven years and probably much more than that, and what do you do?

You get distracted!

So, let's go back a few steps. You were searching online how to make money and you stumbled on this book. I explained to you in the title that this is 'the slow and effective way' to make money in a world gone bananas. You paid for this book (thank you very much), and now that you have this knowledge in your hands, you're flicking through the pages thinking: "uhh, this is boring!".

Well, let me tell you: making money is usually not an exciting exercise, it's hard work, well-executed that adds value. It's a number of steps that you take to MAKE MONEY, it's going through paperwork, negotiating prices, making products or providing a service.

Please, just get this point and re-focus: we're not here to have FUN, we're here to WORK and WORK HARD so we can MAKE MONEY which will then allow us to buy time/experiences/security that we wouldn't otherwise have.

Before you go on, think about this point, make a note for yourself that this is an important chapter and implement as many of the points as possible and even add your own. Remember, this is more a manual than a leisurely read, I'm telling you HOW to make money, and a lot of it.

!!! END OF THE PAUSE !!!

Trade shows, exhibitions and similar events

These are tricky and depend a lot on your industry.

If you're a manufacturer of food products and you can go to an exhibition where there will be hundreds of customers coming to buy food from your stall, you certainly want to take part in these events. On the other hand, if you manufacture industrial goods and you know that the exhibition stand will cost £10,000 and you might not make a single sale, then perhaps you should consider something else.

Trade shows are great places to be, I really do like them and I've never sold anything through them, except when I was working in the food sector. They can also be very expensive, take a lot of resources, a lot of preparation, and yield minimal results.

In the B2B sector I would say that, trade shows are useful if supported by other activities such as:

- Preparing for the show months in advance and publicising your company attendance
- Having a focus product/application and use the trade show to demonstrate the product to the customers (but you need to have interested customers to begin with)
- Personally calling and inviting customers to your stand
- Making your stand look attractive and memorable
- Minimising the impact on your day-to-day business

Obviously, you'll also need to have a system to keep track of events, see how many leads you get at each event, have a box with everything you need, and so on.

Customers' folder, Outlook and general folders

Everything that you need and nothing that you don't.

Repeat with me: everything that you need and nothing that you don't.

Ending up with a messed-up folder system is useless. If you have too much information, within a few months or years, your server/Cloud folder becomes a pit of long-forgotten things... not exactly a well-oiled machine.

What you probably want is a customers' folder with quotes and estimates that you have sent, projects, prices, bespoke items, and similar information. Ideally, you'll file important emails in this folder since you don't want to use Outlook as an archive.

On this point:

1. You receive an email/letter
2. **You process it**
3. Then you either:
    a. File it in the appropriate folder on the Cloud/server
    b. Delete it

Having an inbox with 10,000 emails is insane, it should have a maximum of twenty emails and none older than three months. If something is in your inbox for longer than three months either:

- Put a date in your calendar to return to that email and deal with it (you might be waiting for something else to happen)
- Give up: notify the customer/supplier that this isn't happening anytime soon and to be in touch again in twelve months' time

This kind of approach should go for every file, photo, product specification, price-list, model, 3D model, idea, everything. You should literally 'process' things, get them sorted, and then put the information in the right folder. Again, a boring administration task which will help in the long term.

Final thoughts on the sales and marketing systems

The importance of these systems cannot be understated: your business needs them. Very often, in the early days of your business you will feel that certain things aren't necessary, that they're an overcomplication, that you can keep everything written down on a piece of paper on your desk.

While this might be true for the first few weeks or months when you have everything clear in your mind, but as your business grows, the complexity starts to grow exponentially and soon you'll lose track, and this is when mistakes start to happen, information is lost and weeks and months are wasted.

The main reason, for example, why people don't put a document control system in place is because it is perceived (and it is) a hassle. The reason why people use Excel rather than a CRM is because installing and using one is a hassle (it might take a few hours to get it fully functional).

Always preoccupied with the urgent we forget to take care of the important and, when we have the time, we can't be bothered. This is the real battle that you have to fight with yourself when you're getting into Level 3 of your business and wealth creation.

Finally, to avoid a book of thousands of pages, I'm passing over many of these topics. You could spend weeks on each one of them: how to put a newsletter together, how to organise a trade show, how to implement a DCS, how to organise a sales pipeline.

The message I want you to take from this is:

- Start building your systems early
- Keep in mind that you might want to expand
- Keep them modular
- Have a grand vision of what your business will be
- Start to build for grandeur from the beginning

The accounting, financial and paperwork systems

As we're establishing a set of procedures to deal with sales and marketing, we also have to think about complying with laws, regulations, taxes and so on. You can look at this aspect in two different ways:

- As a chore that you must do well to avoid fines (and save money)
- As a way to keep track of what's really going in your business

Accounting and finance

There are hundreds of books, courses, and tutorials about double entry accounting, how to raise capital from venture capitalists and such things, which are good and nice except that, what you really need to know at the beginning is: "what should I do first?". We'll cover this here.

The first step is to get a good accountant, check for reviews and make sure you have discussed with them how much they'll charge you, what you need to do, what kind of services they provide, and so on.

In regard to the software, you can ask your accountant if they can suggest any specific software. Some people use Sage, which is quite comprehensive but also complex; personally, I like to use Xero which I find quite intuitive.

Once you've got your accountant set up (probably at the beginning once you open the company) and you have a Xero account, the next step is to open a business account with your bank (or a separate standard account if you're in the tax free/sole trader period).

Finally, depending on the bank, you can synchronise your bank account with your accounting software so that, every time you spend or receive money, that transaction is not only listed in your bank account but also automatically imported into your accounting system.

The next step is then to make sure you've got a scanner and a folder called accounting which could be structured like this:

- **Accounts**
  - **Bills**
    - 2020
      - June
      - July
  - **Invoices**
    - Same as 'Bills'
  - **Purchase-Orders-Sent**
    - Same as 'Bills'
  - **Purchase-Orders-Received**
    - Same as 'Bills'
  - **VAT-Returns**
  - **Bank Details**

Bills: contains all the receipts (email order confirmations, PDFs, scanned copies of physical receipts) associated with your business. Everything that you buy for your business should be bought through the card associated with your business. Most of the time you might be able to buy what you need online, however, when you go to a shop and purchase something, keep the receipt, write a note on the back with the date and what it is, and as soon as possible, possibly the same day, 'process it': scan it and file it in the appropriate 'Bill's subfolder.

Invoices: contains all the invoices that you have given to customers.

Purchase-Orders-Sent: to keep track of what you have sent to your suppliers

Purchase-Orders-Received: self-explanatory

VAT-Returns: if you trade above a certain limit, you'll have to register for, and also have to charge, VAT. At the same time, if you buy from suppliers in your own country and then export a lot, it makes sense to register for VAT since you can claim everything back.

Bank Details: you really should have a standard document called 'Company and Bank Details' that you can send to your customers rather than relying on 'flying numbers' on random documents.

At the end of the period (every three months, every month or every year) you then go through all the money in and money out and, for each, you need a bill/receipt to file into your accounting software. For this reason it's very important to keep on top of the accounting as much as possible and do it on a weekly/monthly basis rather than leaving it until the end of the year: the last thing you want is to have a big pro-

ject coming in, little time, and hundreds of documents/invoices to process.
But you'll probably procrastinate and end up in that situation at least once before learning the lesson.

Finance and ownership

Finally, in terms of finance, as a small company that's just getting established you don't really need to know much, unless you have an innovative idea and want to raise capital.

Instinctively, I've always been averse to the idea of 'raising capital' because, in order to do that, you usually forfeit ownership of your company. When it comes to your company, the last thing you want is to dilute ownership (shares). Your company may not amount to much, it may be a small start-up with a dubious future, you may need the skills but not have the money and want to bring a partner in.

My advice is: DON'T.

If you're working so hard to build your business and you've got to this point, in your heart you probably know that, with a little bit of luck your business could grow to £200,000 in a few years, £1,000,000 in less than ten years and, if you're really good, go above £10,000,000 within fifteen to twenty years.

Now, if in 2020 you give a partner (that you've only known for two years and who has got some skills) 30% of your shares to get them on board, you're effectively giving away £3,000,000 or more, depending on how good you are. Does that seem like a sensible idea?

Let's explore this in detail in the next section.

The ownership/ideas/work system

At the beginning, and during the initial phases of your business, the temptation to involve other people (friends, colleagues, relatives) will be there and it will be very strong. You have a vision, an idea, and you believe in YOUR idea and you want other people to believe in it too. From your point of view, it makes sense for other people to join and be passionate about this because you can clearly see that:

- You can all become financially independent
- You can all make some money
- And with luck and hard work, you can all make a lot of money

However, as you've probably gathered from reading this book so far, making money and growing wealth isn't something that everybody will want to do because, very often, there's a heavy price to pay.

Making money is the coalescence of practical acts implemented consistently to generate value. As noted at the beginning of the book, many people want to enjoy the end result of this process, but don't want to go through the process itself. It might be because they have a different view of life, it might be because they're very busy with their own plans, it might be because they lack the ability to focus.

It is not a fault, since everybody is different, and you shouldn't judge or begrudge people that don't embrace your start-up idea. At the same time, you should also be very consistent with yourself: the business is yours, that's it. It doesn't belong to an early business partner who put minimum effort in, it doesn't belong to the clever scientist who could add a lot of value to your business through their ideas, and it certainly doesn't belong to an investment banker.

You own the business and you should never let it go, not even 0.1% of it, and that's exactly why I gave 100% to my wife!

What you'll need to consider when you **evaluate** your business are things like:

- Your turnover
- Your marketing, sales, accounting, production systems, and structures
- Your brand and reputation
- The potential for growth

but above all:

the very fact that you started the business.

Let me expand on this. In order to start and grow your business to the point where it is now, you will have erased one or two years of your life, if not more by working Saturdays, Sundays, holidays, evenings, early mornings etc. It's almost impossible to put a value to that.

Many people will have great idea on things that can be done, on better ways to do what you're doing, on how to improve the production process of your product or the way you position it on the market. You need to take those ideas and try them out, don't resist ideas for the sake of it. At the same time, as long as you are the one implementing it through your own system (your business), the value generated by the implementation of the idea is yours and yours alone.

If you sit down in a quiet room and write down a 'to do list' to improve your business, you can easily come up with a hundred things you could do, so really, most of the time, you won't need suggestions. These are always welcomed, but more often than not, the value they add is minimal since most of them are quite obvious and lack the insight you have into your own business.

What counts is the implementation, what counts is that, after eight hours working in your job, you go back home and work another three hours on your business, sometimes on very boring stuff.

Also remember that it's YOUR idea and you can't expect other people to subscribe to your idea when you still have to prove that it will work. Once it's working, it will be too late for them to join as owners, so they can be suppliers that offer you a service, consultants that you'll pay a fixed amount to, or employees that can do a great job for your company, but certainly not shareholders.

So, as you move from Level 2 to Lever 3, keep this in mind, keep it simple and keep 100% of the ownership, even if it means growing slower and taking longer to get things done; in the medium-long term you will be happier and more productive.

The production/delivery system

Depending on your business, you might have a production line with parts to assemble and put together (so you'll need a Bill of Materials – BOM) where it's very important to keep track of where you buy things from and keep a list of suppliers.

You might also be in a business where you buy and sell things, so again another system will be required to keep track of all of this.

In any case, you want to put together procedures and systems which are specific to your business such as:

- Codified list of ingredients and trusted suppliers
- BOM with suppliers and notes on which ones can be improved
- Pricing for all these elements

This part can be so specific to your process that going into too much detail here doesn't make sense.

Managing complexity

At this point, you're probably realising that starting a business while living, putting together all these systems and having a full-time job is quite challenging. Not only because of the sheer amount of work that you will have to carry out, but also because of the many different things and tasks you will have to tend to: sales, marketing, delivery, production, accounting, family life, personal life, your job, car maintenance, shopping and so on.

Now, if you're a perfectionist, that's the end for you, you'll never be able to follow this strategy to start your own business, because it's simply impossible. So, you'll have to evolve and learn to manage complexity and make compromises.

Throughout this book I've always emphasised the importance of hard work, doing things properly, thinking about the systems and the long-term objectives, and so on. At this point, we need to consider two particularly important principles:

- The best should not be the enemy of the good
- Lose control, go with the flow, but keep an eye on the lighthouses

<u>The best should not be the enemy of the good</u>

I'm finding myself in this position right now and it's very frustrating.

My company website is 'good enough' and, thanks to it, I'm getting a decent amount of business. However, before approaching a new sector with a new range of products, I really wanted to improve the website and make it 'perfect'. Having worked in web design, my standard for 'perfect' is quite high which means that I was asking a lot of my web designer.

However, a mix of changing commitments, priorities and technical issues means that the website isn't ready yet and I'm starting to stress out: my plan was to approach this sector with a new and shiny website, but this still looks months away, so should I:

- Wait for the website to be 100% ready and then start the sales activities
- Start the sales activities now and ACCEPT the fact that the long-dreamed-of new website will probably take another four months?

The answer to any businessman is clear: proceed now, learn from the mistake in timing, and move on.

In this decision there are two fundamental truths.

The first one is that the best (the ideal website, product, prototype) should not be the enemy of the good (an unpolished but functional website, a product that works), so you shouldn't wait for things to be perfect, otherwise you might never start.

The second lesson is that, as a businessperson, you need to always consider the timing and how long things will really take.

<u>Lose control, go with the flow, but keep an eye on the lighthouses</u>

Given the number of things you'll have to manage, you will eventually lose control: your main job will demand you to work overtime, at the same time you will be in the middle of a marketing revamp and then a big project comes in.

At those times it's important to learn to go with the flow which basically means:

- Cut all non-essential activities
- Focus on the core activities that need to be done and done now
- Postpone anything that can be postponed and don't even think about it

It will feel a little bit like your raft has sunk, you're in the middle of a storm, you're swimming and you're trying to get to the lighthouse: as long as you get there, you can then stop on some solid rocks (cash generated by the projects) and wait for the storm to pass before restarting your travel.

Managing complexity

So, managing complexity really boils down to:
- Acceptance that sometimes reality isn't what we want it to be
- Laser-focus on what is important (your key objectives)
- Delegation and timing awareness

Mind your business

The final section of this chapter on Level 3 of the business is: 'Mind your business'. As your business starts to grow, you might be tempted by your own ideas or by others to start to follow some other businesses, be it the sale of dog food, or investing in renovation of properties, cryptocurrencies, or providing insulation to homes. There are millions of business ideas and, when your business starts to grow **not as quickly and as much as you thought it would**, the temptation to jump ship and follow some other business ideas might grow.

At this point remind to yourself to: 'mind your business'.

The world is full of money, some of it has your name of it, but a big chuck does not, so focus on your business and *your* money.

With some RARE exceptions, when you see an opportunity in a sector that you don't know, the opportunity you see either:

- Does not exist, it's just your ignorance of the market that make it seem like an opportunity
- Has already been implemented, so the big profits you think you can make, are much more limited and you're already behind the competition

Obviously, in some cases, you might have a great idea and it would be absurd not to pursue it. However, after you've spent the last three years building your business, is it really a clever idea to change now?

Summary

We've seen how it's possible to run your own business alongside your main job, we've then looked at your product and service and at how to attract customers, and finally we've reviewed some of the main systems that you should have in your company and how to keep them in order and under control.

What I hoped to achieve in this chapter was to give you a practical understanding of things that need to be done early on to avoid chaos later down the line. Most of these are about keeping a consistent production/service/delivery so that your customers know what to expect. At this point, when you're at Level 3, you might start to look at things like ISO 9001 certification which will be a great guideline to standardise your processes; at the same time, you first need to be sure that those processes are really working. So, at the beginning, keep organised and flexible and build some flexibility into your systems so that they don't bog you down.

Easier said than done.

Chapter 11 – The art of selling

Everything there is to know about selling and sales has already been written and said, so, again, this chapter will be a summary of known ideas and practical tips mixed with some philosophical insights.

The importance of sales

This cannot be overstated:

>no sales = no money = no business.

If you have no sales, you don't have a business and you're fooling yourself if you think otherwise. You can have the best systems in place, the best marketing, the best product, and still close your business if you don't sell enough. That's the hard truth about business. Not everybody has large shoulders to keep a business afloat for years until it reaches a break-even point and, as a new business you have two main priorities:

- Minimising expenditures
- Maximising sales

As much as possible you want to **get money in**, and you want to spend only what is strictly necessary since that is **money going out**.

You might have the best possible shop, an amazing location, an innovative product, the best software ever, but if you can't sell it, if you don't sell it, if you don't LEARN how to sell, that's it. It will end up in a bonfire of expenses and money going out.

In some countries there's a strange attitude towards selling and making money in general. Being a salesperson can be perceived as a negative thing and trying to make money can also be associated with evil, greed and some other negative ideas. Now, if you're in those countries or you were raised there, you need to recognise this early on and embrace sales as a mean to freedom, wealth creation and progress.

In any organisation, it isn't the accountant who creates value (at best, they manage value), it isn't the production operative who puts parts together, it isn't even the engineer or the scientist who are coming up with great ideas… it's the salesperson who, constantly looking for opportunities, finds where to place the products and the services, how to promote them and how to connect with the customers.

You need to learn to sell if your business requires interaction with customers. Obviously, if you're selling skates online with no interaction, you probably think you don't need to know how to sell, except that you actually do:

- How can you negotiate with your suppliers if you can't sell them the idea of your future sales?
- How can you deal with people within your growing business if you can't sell them the idea of working for you?
- How can you negotiate with other businesspeople if you have no idea of how to sell?

This means that, before shunning sales because you "don't like it", you should learn how to sell and get some direct experience in selling. Get a part-time job before you start your business - or even after you've started - to learn how to sell.

Practical selling

You're running your business (you might have just started), you have some products in your shop, some online and some that you sell to other business via projects and agreements. Now you need to know what to do next.

Answering emails

It goes without saying that emails are going to be one of your main sales tools in 2020, and yet many people get them wrong. Let's say you receive an enquiry from your website asking if such and such product can be used to do A, B and C. You want to match the writing style of your customer.

If they are formal, you will be formal; if they are informal, you can be semi-formal; if they write long paragraphs you will answer with a long explanation; if they are straight to the point, you will be straight to the point.

Things I tend to look out for are:

- The style and how they open and close the email
- If they like longwinded sentences or short and to the point
- If it sounds hurried or as if the customer is still at the evaluation stage
- Specific words or expressions that I can recycle in my answers (use the style of your customers!)
- Use of I, you or plural pronouns to understand if they are focused on themselves or otherwise

Let me give you some good and bad examples of emails so that, rather than learning the hard way, you can have some good templates to take inspiration from.

Good example of a formal/semi-formal email

Dear Nichole,

Thank you very much for your email.
[Always thank the person for the email]

After going through your email regarding our Product A, I have some questions to better understand what we can do for you:
[Never give a price straight away, always ask some questions to clarify, you want to start a conversation]

- How are you planning to use Product A?
- What would you like to achieve?
- What do you prefer in terms of style?
  [Here's where you actually do the selling: by asking open ended questions you let the customer tell you what they want so that you can use your products to satisfy that need]

Also, since you like our Product A, have you thought about Complement A, B and C?
[Here you try to upsell and get the customer to look at other accessories]

Most people get Complement B, when going for Product A.
[They're not alone, it's a tested product]

Please let me know a little bit more so we can help you.

Kind Regards,

Name Surname

          ***

Some things to note:

- Opening and closing of the email
- Structure and use of bullet points
- Talking about "YOU" (them)
- Open ended questions: questions that cannot be answered as YES/NO, GOOD/BAD but need the customer to elaborate
- Trying to sway the conversation towards additional products/services

Bad example of a Formal/Semi-formal email

Dear Nichole,

I have received your email and I really think the best solution is our Product B, rather than our Product A, which is a lower end and lower quality alternative.

I have been selling these for years and our Product A gives only trouble, so my strong suggestion is to go for Product B.

The price for it is £550 but I can drop it to £500 if you place the order by the end of play tomorrow.

I'm at the office only until midday tomorrow, so please keep that in mind.

I'm happy to give you my opinion also on other products if you need.

Best,

Name

***

Some things to note:

- Not thanking for the email
- I, I, I, my, I … this person is thinking about himself, he doesn't really care about Nichole
- Slandering one's own products is never a good idea
- Perhaps Nichole could only afford Product A!
- Giving the price straight away, with no commitment, no discussion, it then becomes a price war with other people Nichole has written to
- Why did he reduce the price? Pressure selling to get the order soon: this person is desperate

Now, to the inexperienced eye, these two emails might seem similar and the second might even seem to the point and, while sometimes this might work, in most cases you will lose customers and/or create a disconnect.

Good example of an informal and to the point email

Hi Tom,

Thanks for the message.
[Always thank them for the message]

Sure, we have had a look and it seems you're in luck: we still have one Product A left in stock! Congratulations!
[Here we start with a positive word, 'sure', and then we point out to scarcity with a joke]

Attached, you can find some photos of how it looks and the technical datasheet.
[This is where you make the customer want to put his hand on the product]

How should we proceed? I'm in all day tomorrow, so feel free to pop in to get it.
[Asking if Tom wants to place an order and give a wide availability for collection plus an assumption to close: you assume he will come in to get (buy) it]

Hope this helps and talk soon,

Name

***

Some things to notice are:

- Thanking for the message, even if they're a good customer already
- Always use positive language
- Rather than pressure selling, give some friendly hints about stock level
- Do that extra work to conclude the sale
- Close the sale, ask for the next steps
- Close the email in a friendly fashion

Bad example of an informal and to the point email

Hi Tom,

I have looked for Product A and I have only one left in stock.

As I said weeks ago, I'm not going to order more so when it's gone that's it. Good luck finding it anywhere else.

All the best,

Name

***

Self-explanatory

It's not rare to see that kind of badly written, non-structured, blobs of rudeness and badly masked attempts of pressure selling and, if you're an experienced salesperson, you'll probably ask yourself: "what were these people thinking?".

Exercise – Tips for good emails

Some tips on writing good sales emails (and emails in general):

- Check your spelling: activate the spell check on Outlook and Office in general – NOW
- Learn to write with a focus on the other person (use YOU more than I, YOUR more than MY/MINE)
- Use bullet lists, make sure the text is legible, use fonts which are legible and big enough
- Keep it simple and to the point, and, if you really have to write something which is long, make sure it flows and that it makes sense
- Re-read your email and check if you're saying anything crazy or anything which could be badly perceived
- Re-read again, check the subject, check who you're sending it to, check if you're copying anyone else
- Remove the I, my, mine and rephrase things so that the focus is the customer, what they want and need
- Send it

Answering the phone

Yes, eventually it will ring, and you will have to speak with someone. Before that happens learn this sentence:

"Good morning/afternoon [name of your business], how can I help?"

You don't answer by saying: "Hello, who's calling?", "Hi, who is it?" etc. You confirm who you are, clearly, and ask how you can help.

Past this sentence your potential customer (or supplier – other people will try to sell you things and some might add value) will start to talk and at this point:

- The line might be bad: if this is the case, say it! Nothing is more unproductive than a conversation on an unstable phone line
- You have no idea who they are/what their name is: ask for some details such as company name, person's name, best number to call them back if the line breaks
- Never stop your customers or interrupt them: let them talk. The more they talk, the stronger their relationship with you. You create a relationship by active listening and giving feedback using words and phrases such as: "OK", "Yes, I see" etc.
- Don't stay silent the whole time
- Ask open questions to encourage them to talk more
- Try to agree a next step (usually a meeting or an email)

Usually, during your first conversation over the phone with a customer, what the customer wants to do really is to understand who they're dealing with.

In all your communications, the feeling you want to transmit is that of the:

Unbiased, reliable and relatable professional consultant

Keep this expression clear in your head. As the business owner and the main salesperson in your business you are:

- **Unbiased**: you are really listening and trying to understand what your customer needs. You do that because you really want to solve their problem/need. At this stage, forget about selling and focus all your energy in understanding the other person's point of view
- **Reliable**: talk calmly and slower than you would face to face. You want your words to have weight and you want people to take you seriously. Practice talking with friends and family about your products and services until you give a feeling of reliability.
- **Relatable**: at the same time, you want to sound friendly, you need to create that connection. So, at the same time as you are establishing your credibility you want to keep a door open to get the conversation on a friendlier tone so that the customer, who's looking to talk with an expert, knows that you are a friendly expert.

- **Professional**: in anything you say, you must be professional. Don't talk badly about other companies, don't say things which could sound strange. Don't discuss politics, religion, sex, race or any other subjective topic. You're a professional who is looking to offer a product and the customer is not your friend at the pub.
- **Consultant**: look at yourself as a sales doctor. The customer has a disease (a non-energy efficient house, a broken car, a broken laptop) and you have to use your knowledge, skills, tools as medicines to cure this problem. Nothing more, nothing less.

Sometimes you can go through books and only find a certain interesting and useful concept. The concept we just expressed is one of those powerful ones. If you can master this approach, attitude, mental state, everything else will be easier.

It doesn't make sense to try and implement an elevator pitch or a trial close (research them now!) when you're doing a double jack-knife twist if you haven't the right attitude. Take a moment and think of the times you've been sold something by an: **unbiased, reliable and relatable professional consultant.**
And then try to be one.

Prospecting via phone: cold calling

This is the dreaded one but sometimes it's necessary. Let's assume that your business sells coffee machines to pubs, restaurants and coffee shops and then you provide service and maintenance, coffee, and spare parts. Is the owner of a coffee shop going to look for a £5,000 coffee machine to replace his £3,000 coffee machine before he needs to? Probably not!

So, you might have the best possible website, with the best possible marketing and you will still need to cold call. You might decide to send letters to all the pubs and restaurant owners in your area and they might end up forgotten on a desk, lost or directly into the junk.

You might then decide to send emails, tens of thousands of them and realise that it's not working, because coffee shops don't really check their emails.
Finally, you might have a great idea and decide to talk with people, start making phone calls and start making money.

There are different ways to start a conversation and that will depend on the customers that you are targeting.

If your customers are pubs, restaurants, and small shops, then you can probably try to talk directly with the owner so you should create an elevator pitch that you repeat over and over, with some small variations, until you get something that works. Whenever you do this, the important thing is DO NOT RUSH, let the other person understand your name and where you're calling from, establish some sort of connection, and say what you're offering.

If your customers are bigger companies with fifty or more people, then trying to talk with the relevant person straight away can be difficult, so you need to do a little bit of research (using their website, LinkedIn) and use this trick:

- **Secretary**: "Good morning, such and such, how can I help/redirect your call?"
- **You** (in a **very bored and slow tone**): "Hi, good morning, this is Frank from Bolts and Nuts Unlimited. I'm looking to send some marketing material to the production department, where can I send it to?"
- **Secretary**: "You can send it info@suchandsuch.com" (or, if you're lucky, a person's email address)
- **You** (still very bored): "OK thanks, I've got it, who should I address it to?"
- **Secretary**: "You can address it to Matthew, he looks after those things" OR "Just send it there, it will then be sent to the relevant person"
- **You**: "OK, thank you very much, have a great day!"

By using this approach, you obtain a number of things:

- You have spoken at least once with the gate keeper and tried to connect with them
- Possibly got a personal email address
- Got the first touch with the company

Obviously, if you can keep the conversation going and ask them about the latest news you've seen on their website, about the general business or who they use as suppliers, you might even gather more information.

Now, the bigger the organisation, the more complicated it will be to talk with the people in charge of a department, so you might want to try and talk with different people in the organisation and see if you can get someone on board with your idea. Finally, when prospecting via cold calling, it's a numbers game, which means that you can't expect to do ten phone calls a day and be successful. You need to aim for large volumes of calls, between thirty and one hundred a day, for weeks and weeks to generate some substantial revenue.

Some will
Some won't
So what?
So, who's next?

Prospecting via social media and emails

If you use LinkedIn you've most likely received messages asking you to connect and, soon after you've connected, a request to discuss things you don't know about, or are not interested in. So, the first step is: don't be annoying and don't message everyone. You've got a powerful tool that tells you everything you need to know about a certain person, you know that they work in finance, that they work for a bank, that they've been there for the last ten years… so why would you send a message about the bulk supply of sugar?

On the other hand, if you use LinkedIn and other similar social media platforms to connect with the relevant people (and always say why you think it's worth them connecting with you, what is the professional reason for doing so), this can be a very powerful tool.

A typical message might be something like: "Good morning Jess, I noticed that you work as CAD designer for Such-and-such Ltd. We use this profile to share information on CAD innovation, it might be interesting to connect and share some experiences?"

As for phone calls, this will require you to send hundreds, if not thousands, of messages. Again, what you're looking for is a 'breach', a way to connect with a business or customer and provide them with your products and services.

You're not looking to get a 100% response rate, if you're lucky you'll get a 1% success rate, but you want your name out there, you want the 'first touch' to be delivered in a professional fashion to as many people as possible and, above all, you want to persist for weeks and months.

It's similar for emails, and again, we should think about numbers, personalisation, and a personal touch.

The reality of prospecting

It's all nice and well until you actually start prospecting. Armed with your newly acquired knowledge and a perfectly written script, you pick up the phone and you call and:

- Nobody answers
- The person on the other end of the phone hangs up on you
- They listen silently and say to send an email to info@suchandsuch.com which will be soon deleted with one click
- They say they're not interested even before you can say exactly what you have to offer

Welcome to the real world of prospecting and selling, where busy businesspeople know what they need better than you do, where customers don't have the time to listen to you, where the gate keeper's job is to politely tell you to go away, and where everybody wants to sell but nobody wants to be sold to.

This is why I said that, ideally, your first approach should be to 'be found by the customer' rather than 'actively find customers'. At the same time, I emphasised that, often, you can't simply rely on being found but you will also have to do prospecting.

So now that we know the harsh reality of prospecting, what can we do about it? A lot!

First, remember that you're "eating frogs" and that it's better done "early in the morning", which basically means as soon as possible. Don't postpone prospecting, get it ticked off as early as possible, and do a little bit every day, as soon as your marketing, branding and business is presentable.

Second, you want to really understand what's happening. Don't just make a script and repeat it like a parrot thousands of times over with no changes. Try variations, see what works and what doesn't, and, above all, record your conversations and critically think about what you can do differently.

Third, enjoy the process! After all, you might be closed in a room doing something very boring, but instead you have the chance to know hundreds and thousands of people, make friends, make connections, get new ideas, give new ideas.

Fourth, give yourself ambitious targets of calls/e-mails per day. You need to be BUSY (remember busyness) and finally, you need to have:

A VERY LONG LIST TO PROCESS!

<u>The list</u>
This is important

Let us imagine two people: Vanessa and Jenny.

Vanessa has spent the weekend preparing a list of all the businesses she will call the following week. She's got a list of four hundred companies, with email addresses, phone numbers, some LinkedIn contacts, and some comments on what these businesses do.

Jenny, on the other hand, has spent the weekend focusing on improving her marketing, making it very nice and shiny with a social media campaign. She also plans to call and email companies during the coming week, but her approach is to do the search and the calling at the same time, so she'll look for potential businesses, phone them up, send an email, and then move on to search for the next potential customer.

Which one is going to have better results? Vanessa, no doubt.

Why?

You have your first week of holiday and you're planning to use this for your own business. You're full of energy and it's Monday morning. You pick up the phone thinking: "I'm going to make this happen".

Now, if you're Vanessa, you know that there are four hundred companies on your list, that four hundred divided by five working days in a week means eighty companies per day (which is a lot of people to contact). You also realise that on Friday, many companies finish early and that not everybody will pick up the phone: this means that, even going at full speed, you'll probably barely fit them all in and you have no time to lose.

On the other hand, if you're Jenny, you don't have a clear objective. You might want to contact eighty companies per day, but you might have more stress than Vanessa because you're searching and then being rejected, and then searching again, and your target feels unreachable.

Vanessa makes the first five phone calls, all the gate keepers are quite rude and don't give anything away. Vanessa makes a note to send a general presentation email to info@suchandsuch.com and moves on QUICKLY (there are still seventy-five to go and time is running out!).

On the other hand, after her first five rejections, Jenny starts to look more carefully at the prospective clients' websites and tries to understand them better: basically, she's scared of the rejection.

At the end of the first day, Vanessa has contacted seventy businesses and Jenny has contacted twenty-five. At the end of the day, Vanessa is tired but satisfied since her 57th and 65th call resulted in an appointment.

At the end of the same day, Jenny feels very depressed because it took her a long time to find good businesses and, when she called them, none were interested.

Repeat this for the whole week, months and years, and you'll see why some people say cold calling is dead and some other people say that it works.

What should we learn from this?

That ideally you want to separate these three phases:

- Organising the list of people/businesses you want to call (Preparation)
- Calling them to send material, arrange meetings, arrange a visit (Prospection)
- Carrying out the actual meeting, discussing things via email (Sales)

In bigger organisations, these are tasks that are assigned to different people. For example, they might purchase bulk data from a data supplier, someone will then have to phone the customers up to organise a meeting, and finally the shiny salesperson will go there and have a meeting.

You don't have £20,000 to buy bulk data of contacts, you don't have anyone working for you, so you'll have to do all three of them yourself.... but keep the roles separate.

A time for calling and a time for the rest

Imagine you've just completed the first ten phone calls, most of them have asked you to send some brochures to info@suchandsuch.com; one wanted an offer for ten units of Product A. It's 10:30 in the morning and you started at 9:00. Now what do you do?

- You continue calling because you have another seventy companies to call?
- You spend thirty minutes putting an offer together?
- You spend one hour sending emails to these ten companies?

Obviously, you continue calling. During the day people usually work from 9:00 to 12:00 and from 14:00 to 17:00.

Before 9:00, you don't know who you'll find in the office; between 12:00-14:00, you don't know the lunch arrangements; after 17:00, you don't know if you'll find people to talk to.

So, while nothing stops you from calling and prospecting at those times, **your golden hours** are from 9:00 to 12:00 and from 14:00 to 17:00. You might call early in the morning, late in the evening or at the weekend and find very dedicated business owners working overtime, but those are exceptions.

You can send the urgent emails out at lunchtime and the rest after 17:00 or even during the weekends, but **do things at the right time**.

It goes without saying that, calling people for hours and hours can be tiring, so make sure you get plenty of rest the night before.

Sales 101: practical, to the point, no fluff

Having been in sales for over ten years and having read more than twenty books on the subject, I can say for sure that there's no single book or author that can give you 'the truth'. Someone's suggestions will apply very well to selling cars or door-to-door selling, but won't work if you're trying to sell complicated financial products; you might want to use some pressure selling at a food trade fair but certainly not when you're taking part in a tender and so on. In these pages, I'll report my view of different selling topics, which will certainly be shaped by the sector I've been working in.

Attitude: external

One day I was in France talking with a sales manager from another company. The guy had the most anonymous face you can imagine, he wasn't a handsome man but was always well-dressed and was one of the best salespeople I've ever met.

After a few days at a trade fair with him, I started to ask myself: "Why am I so comfortable talking with this person?", "Why do people stick to him while they shun the other younger and more energetic salesperson?".

The industry I was working in is mainly male-dominated with many big, strong boys with some huge egos, shoulders and muscles. Company directors, assuming chief engineers, regulators and so on, all full of testosterone, all trying to be the biggest gorilla in the room.

In this very hostile and threatening environment there was a very smart, non-threatening, soft-spoken and professional average-looking guy who you could trust, because he wasn't a 'competitor' in this ego arena. He was, and still is, a very successful salesperson, the go-to person, the one who's been in the field forever, and the one who'll listen to what you say and guide you, without you even realising what he's doing.

At the end of the night I bluntly asked him if he was doing that on purpose, he smiled and said with a French accent: "It doesn't matter how YOU, as a salesperson, feel; what matters is how the other person feels, so that they buy, you sell, and then you feel good on the French riviera when you're being yourself".

Many people who start out in selling try to be too boisterous because, for some odd reason, that is how overconfident salespeople have been depicted; some others try to be 'yes men' and end up seeming 'slimy'.

As a salesperson, your interest is in understanding the other person, what they want or need, and how you can guide them towards the right buying decision and, sometimes, that means you have to act a part.

Guiding, in selling, means asking the right questions such as:

- What do you think of this colour?
- Did you know that you could use this also during rainy days?
- Do you prefer to make a bigger investment now and have a better return, or to keep the initial expense low but it will end up costing more in the long term?
- How do you feel about this investment? What other options have you considered?

And, you're not asking the question just because you want to guide them (otherwise any nodding or expression of agreement you use will be clearly fake and will create a strange atmosphere) but because you really NEED to understand to be in the best position to give sound advice.

Attitude: internal

Sales is also an internal game. As a salesperson, you're really an athlete: you have to train yourself hard to perform well. You have to study, you have to read books about selling (go online, buy four or five at once, read them, forget them, read them again in a few years), you have to practice, you have to keep physically and mentally fit, you have to be punctual, precise, cordial, focused, persuasive, reasonable, able to close the sale but not pushy. Good luck!

These are the reasons why I really like selling, it's not simply the reward of winning the sale for your business, it's not the validation that you get from your customers; but it's the dealing with complexity that sales entails and the ability to see the world and its people from another perspective.

I've heard middle-managers saying countless times: "Be in the driving seat", without having a clue why they were failing. As a good salesperson, you can really be in the driving seat, of a car that the customer doesn't know exists, heading to a destination that's not yet clear to them but that they'll love.

So, if you want to be a good salesperson, you should:

- Dress for the job, even if working from home
- Be consistent and accept that you need to process some numbers to get the sales
- Never give up! Many times, you just have to persist, and often, for some strange reason, you'll get the order that will save the day from the very last customer you call
- Balance your life: eat, rest, exercise, sleep, don't burn out (otherwise you lose everything)

- Believe in yourself: if you're experiencing feelings of self-doubt or inadequacy: look at the current leaders around the world, from the East to the West, are they really better than you? Do you believe that? This is not an era for self-doubt.
- Work: you'll have to work, and work hard (making the lists, calling, following up via email, phone calls, voice messages, updating the CRM etc.)

CRM: use it and keep it in order

The CRM is your friend, you really want to use it. When you talk with your customers, note things down about the projects, about what they like, about what they want, phone numbers, addresses, other email addresses of people copied in the emails: you want all the data to be well organised in your CRM for future use and reference.

At the same time, ideally, you want to create a folder structure to keep everything about a customer filed. For my business I have a system like this:

```
Business
    Prospects
        ProspectOne
            Emails
                Received
                Sent
            Projects
            Legal-Agreements
    Customers
        […]
```

In this way, when someone finally buys something, their business moves into the 'Customers' folder, otherwise it stays in 'Prospects'. Also, I only file important emails, such as those with quotes, prices, agreements, and other important things. In this way, Outlook, doesn't become an unusable repository of GBs of junk, but is simply a processing tool.

Obviously, as the business grows, moving to a CRM that allows you to file emails rather than manually having to make folders is a more reasonable practice, but at Level 3 you might not be there yet.

Questions

Being able to ask questions, the right questions, is at the heart of selling, there is no escaping it. Even if your sales model doesn't involve talking with customers (for example if you sell online), you'll still have to 'ask questions' through your website, through the purchasing process, through the menu. It is always about developing a conversation.

There are mainly two types of questions: open and closed. Closed questions can be answered with a simple YES/NO, GOOD/BAD, SAD/HAPPY; open questions encourage the customer to expand their answers and they usually begin with 'how', 'what', and so on. Some examples below:

Closed questions

- Is this too expensive?
  Answer: Yes
- Do you like this model?
  Answer: No
- Have you been here before?
  Answer: No
- Do you want to buy this?
  Answer: No

Closed question should be avoided in the first stages of your sales conversation. At the beginning, you're exploring what the customer wants or needs, so you should ask the same things but in a slightly different way:

- How does this fit with your budget?
  Answer: It's a bit expensive to be honest
- What do you think of this model?
  Answer: I don't like the colour of this model, I'd rather get a yellow one
- Which other shops have you visited?
  Answer: I visited the shop over there and the one next door, but they didn't have what I was looking for.
- So how should we proceed?
  Answer: Let me try this on please

As you can see the open questions usually lead to more information with which you can build the next question and the next question and so on. After a few questions you're actually having a real conversation with your customer, trying to understand the motivations behind their choices and, at the same time, thinking about how you can fulfil that need with your product or service.

Body language, how you dress, and the persona

Do some research on body language, what an open and closed body posture looks like, how you should try to naturally make eye contact, and so on.

If you're sitting at a table, perhaps taking out your laptop to show the customer something, might mean that rather than sitting one in front of each other, you're sitting next to each other (from confrontation to cooperation).

If the customer has his arms crossed (closed language), give them a brochure or a product, so he can open up.

Look at how the customer uses the space, make them comfortable, don't invade their space but, at the same time, don't create an ice wall between you.

Mirror their body language, not in an obvious way, but if you can, do it naturally, when they assume a position, try to assume the same position too: we like to buy from people like us.

How you dress is also important. First of all, you need to be tidy as a salesperson – which doesn't mean that you can't grow a beard, but just don't be untidy. Once you've established this baseline, try to always be dressed appropriately, which means slightly better than your customer but appropriate for the setting.

I still remember once going to a refinery in Eastern Europe with my best dress on and polished shoes and being surrounded by operatives and technicians with their dirty working clothes. I certainly misjudged. In that setting, a more casual style of clothing would've been more appropriate.

At the same time, I still remember a Japanese distributor telling me over a Skype call: "Oh, so you dress very casual at the office" while they had dressed up properly for a business meeting even if it was a virtual one. The sense of shame was great, and, after that, I learnt to dress up smartly when doing business meetings with Japanese people.

Finally, if you have to buy a car, clothes and everything else, while you need something useful and good quality, you don't want to overdo it: if you go to visit a customer (or they come to visit you), you want to project the idea of reliability and professionalism but you don't want them to feel jealous and think: "I'm not going to pay for his expensive car!".

Active listening and not interrupting

I've been to so many sales meetings where the salesperson was interrupting the customers over and over, almost like a battle of ideas, but can you WIN an argument? Somewhere I read that the only argument you win is the one you avoid.
There are only very few people who will actually admit they were wrong, people don't like to 'lose face', we all like to be right and, above all, when we strongly believe we are right, it's very difficult to be convinced of the contrary.

As a clever businessperson, you know that you can be wrong, you realise that any truth is such until proven wrong, you realise that your opinion should change.

Your main job as a salesperson isn't to change the attitudes of fifty year old men or super-self-confident twenty years old models, but your main job is to sell, because the more you sell, the quicker your business will grow and the more wealth you will generate.

So, just remember to practice active listening, when a customer says something wrong do NOT correct them, try to avoid confrontation, allow people to save face, give them a way out and, above all, make sure that it's all their idea.

An example:

- **Customer:** I'd like to get a new PC to do video editing
- **You:** OK, then you're looking at something with a good graphic card, have you thought about Model X?
- **Customer:** Yes, but I prefer Model Y, I think it's got a very good graphic card
  [At this point you know that Model Y's graphic card is really bad, but you don't want to start an argument, so you nod and say:]
- **You:** Yes [start positive!], I see, Model Y is good for video editing for beginners since it hasn't got a separated graphic card. What kind of video editing are you planning to do? Really basic or intermediate?
  [You haven't said "You're wrong, you have no idea", but you've implicitly pointed out that it isn't the best choice and given him a way out]
- **Customer:** Oh, I need to do advanced stuff, you know YouTube, 3D videos, I'm a professional you see
- **You:** Perfect, I can see that! Have you ever thought about Graphic Card XYZ? It's £100 more expensive than Model Y, but it'll allow you to do professional editing for years to come
  [Here you give information as a question, you give a price reference which you think is acceptable, and repeat the word 'professional']
- **Customer:** Oh that sounds nice, let me see the specs

We could write a full encyclopaedia with these kinds of dialogues, but they're quite simple to master once you keep in mind some principles:

- Always keep a positive tone, do NOT start sentences with "NO", "Yes, but", "BUT", "I think"
- Lead the customer to the right conclusions, but do so in the right way
- Give information as a question
- Use the same language as your customer
- Be a consultant, a sales doctor, not someone who wants to win an argument
- Keep the goal in mind: selling
- Have a polite conversation
- Never point out when the customer is wrong (unless strictly necessary)

The greatest salesmen in the world

One of the classics in sales is the book by Og Mandino where the main concept is never giving up, persisting, and trying your best to excel. I find that many of these books are very useful, above all if you can imagine yourself as a certain kind of person and then 'play that role' until you really become it.

For example, you could think of yourself as a professional and friendly sales doctor, who always gives the best advice guiding customers towards the right choices, who is genuinely interested in understanding his customer, the market and the products and, at the same time, you want to refine the art of closing the sale in such a natural way that it isn't even perceived by the customer.

On the other hand, you might want to focus on the relationships that you build with your customers, on the long-term game, on the fact that you want to give an authentic experience.

There are countless combinations, just choose one or two, study the others and play the game.

Conclusion

Selling is an art. It requires you to be clever, it requires you to perceive what the other person is thinking and feeling, it requires you to DECIDE how you react to objections and to your customers in general. It's beyond the scope of this book to teach you how to sell, but I hope that after reading these pages you have realised the importance of studying, learning and practicing this skill, and remember that between 'stimulus' (rejection) and 'response' (you feeling rejected), there is a space, in that space is your freedom to choose to try to overcome the rejection, sell and make money.

On pricing, working hard and making money

One of my favourite operas is *The Beggar's Opera* (in its various versions including the 'Threepenny Opera') which talks about life in the London of 1700. There are many inspiring bits in it about law, love, power, money and trade, and, this one in particular, I feel is quite relevant to this book.
When trying to make money starting from a situation of poverty and need, I think many valuable lessons can be learnt about human nature and trade, and travelling around the world, I have had the good fortune to observe these things first-hand. For this reason, you nowadays get some very clever businesspeople from India, China and 'the developing world': they had to face some huge challenges early on and learn to thrive in a difficult and uncertain environment. Well done to all of them, really!

But let's study some valuable lessons about the nature of work and trade.

Employments[16]

Through all the employments of life
Each neighbour abuses his brother
The making of money means strife
As we rob and we plunder each other

So why blame the bold highway man
Please pity your sister the whore
For we are all after higher pay when
We do it for more and for more
Yes! We do it for more and for more!

The lawyer demands his fat fee
It's certainly fatter than mine
And the priest counts his stipend while he
Tells his beads that his office is divine

For these are the rules of the game
There's no-one does nothing for naught
In high life and low it's the same
You loot and you rob or you've bought
Oh, tether to your stations my dears
Should you work with your hands or your brain
Be like statesmen and prelates and peers
Make sure that your watchword is gain

For a man should be proud of his labour
And industry must be his guide
So grab all you can from your neighbour
As you ride and you ride and you ride
Yes! We ride and we ride and we ride
Ah! We ride and we ride and we ride
For we ride and we ride and we ride

---

[16] John Gay, 'Employments', *The Beggar's Opera*

Exercise: Research and listen to the various versions

Obviously, I'm not suggesting you take this as a moral position when doing business and dealing with money. However, you must be 1,000% aware that, a part of the population (be it your customers, your consultants, your lawyers, your suppliers etc.) will strongly believe in the song above. So, what does this mean in practical terms? Many things that you will understand with time, but above all:

- Always negotiate with suppliers for the best possible prices
- Always try to charge a good price
- The making of money means strife
- Make sure your watchword is gain

MAKE SURE YOUR WATCHWORD IS GAIN

...and on this note we conclude this chapter.

Chapter 12 – The switch

In the last few chapters, we've taken a more practical look at how to actually grow your business. If you've followed these steps and persisted for a few years with the overall plan, you'll now be approaching a situation where:

- You have more than three rental properties with increasing returns and you're consistently overpaying every month/year to reduce the mortgage quicker
- You and your partner might both still be in full-time employment
- You've been able to start your business, put the right systems in place and it's growing year on year
- You've also put aside an emergency fund that will cover six months of expenses
- And last but not least, you're very good at your job and at your business

At this stage (four to ten years into the plan), you might find yourself in this kind of position. This doesn't aim to be an 'optimised view' and the numbers are here just to give you a feeling of how things could work out.

It doesn't make sense to put down specific numbers because much will depend on house prices, your wage, your business, the rental market etc… and I don't want to give you a fairy tale view of what things COULD be, but I want you to learn some basic Excel and do your own calculations.

Your properties

	Your home	**Rental 1**	**Rental 2**	**Rental 3**
Value bought	£120,000	£70,000	£70,000	£70,000
Outstanding mortgage	£70,000	£45,000	£45,000	£45,000
Years left on the mortgage	15	15	15	15
Monthly mortgage payments	£465	£300	£300	£300
Rent coming in	£400	£500	£500	£500
Gross profit (before tax and expenses)	-£65	£200	£200	£200

Your wages (for a couple)

Person 1	£2,300 per month
Person 2	£2,300 per month

Your business (last nine months net profit)

	1	2	3	4	5	6	7	8	9
Gain	£1450	£1650	£1250	£1800	£2700	£600	£2200	£1900	£2400

Your savings

Properties bank account	£7,000
Person 1 bank account	£15,000
Person 2 bank account	£10,000
Business account	£8,000

As with everything in this book, we're talking about what's really feasible in the economy between 2020 and 2030, mainly in advanced economies, with moderate growth, low interest rates, lowish inflation, and so on. We're not expecting property values to double every three years, we're not expecting your business to fly overnight, and we're certainly not expecting you to save hundreds of thousands of pounds in a few years.

I also think that it's EXTREMELY likely that, if you do things properly, save and pay off mortgages, you can be in a much better position than the one above. **It all boils down to Money In and Money Out**.

So, where do you go from here (or similar situations)?

This is what I call 'The Switch', which is somehow like 'The Junction' but at a higher level.

Let's depict the scenario, so we can picture what's happening at this moment in your life.

You're still working full-time at your job because it still pays better than your business and helps you to pay off the mortgages quicker, and so is your partner who's also helping with the business. At the same time, you're collecting rent every month from three properties and keeping in touch with the tenants; the properties are in working order but you know that one of the boilers will need replacement and the roof, eventually, might need replacing in Property 2, so you're trying to save up for those big jobs. Your own business is taking all the rest of your time, and you've maxed out both in terms of time and energy. To grow your business you need to go full-time or, at least part-time, but you really do need two full days per week, from 9:00 to 19:00 to be working flat out on your business. Finally, with all these savings, commitments, mortgages and work, you haven't had a proper holiday in two years, and you're starting to feel exhausted.

You need a change and you need to plan the switch: from being employed to be fully self-employed/reliant on your own business and other sources of income.
It's impossible to say WHEN you should take this step, there are just too many variables:

- You might want to continue as an employee for as long as possible to pay off the mortgages quickly
- You might want to jump quickly because you're losing money by not focusing on your business full-time
- You might want to try and go part-time with your job to maximise the income from both
- You might want to wait for a big project to come in

and so on. This will depend on you and your specific situation, however, there will be a point where it will become impossible to do everything and you'll have to make a choice and decide if you're really serious about your own business OR if you're too scared and will continue to work on someone else's business idea.

As you're approaching this decision, there are several things you can do:

1. Take a holiday and enjoy a break – you've worked hard for this!
2. Try to close one or two mortgages so that you have a steady flow of cash coming in
3. Once that has been done, give an extra push to your own business
4. Try to go part-time or to be a consultant for your present employer, in this way both of you can have a smooth transition
5. And finally, switch

It doesn't matter how long you delay the choice, this is where you wanted to be the whole time, you wanted to be your own boss, do things your own way, have full control of how things are done, have time to spend on your own business, ideas, passions, and so on.

In the worst-case scenario, you can still find another job: you're a highly specialised professional. Also, with the support of your property investment you can be quite confident that you won't starve, and, with the support of your partner, you know that you can actually have a pretty decent life.

Mission Accomplished!

Except, that you are again just at the beginning.

You're now working full-time on your business and, unexpectedly, you have the worst month since starting, you read the news and it seems like a new financial crisis is bubbling, your partner has just been informed that her position is gone, and one of your tenants doesn't pay the rent. Panic sets in.

This was your worst nightmare and it's happening at the worst possible time, however, after a few days of confusion you realise that:

- You've still got money coming thanks to your assets and the decisions you've taken over the course of the previous years
- Your partner will find another job soon
- This morning you've received a request from your website for a project that could bring your company to the next level with a little bit of luck.

You're now fully in the game: you've learnt to walk independently, and now it's time to run towards Level 4 and, with luck and ingenuity, Level 5.

What you were missing was someone to explain to you how to get to this point, in fact, you've often thought: "If I were the owner of such-and-such a business, I would do X, Y and Z and I would be successful, the owner is incompetent". Now you are the owner and you clearly know the way forward, don't you?

You've probably also realised that the owner of such-and-such a business is actually a very capable businessperson and being in business can be quite challenging at times.

Level 4

*Taxes
National
And
International*

'Tis impossible to be sure of any thing but Death and Taxes[17]

---

[17] The Cobbler of Preston by Christopher Bullock (1716)

Chapter 13 – The devil is in the detail

I'm not a national or international accountant, a tax attorney, a company lawyer, a policy-maker nor any of those highly specialised figures who know – and in some cases make – the law of the land and of the foreign lands.

This means that everything that's written in the following pages must be taken as my opinion rather than being relied on to make important decisions: always speak with an accountant, lawyer or advisor on these matters.

The objective of these pages is to give you some food for thought on things you should consider, early on, when starting to structure your wealth. If you're serious about this journey, you should really take some time to familiarise yourself with some laws and legislations in your country because the choices you make early on can affect what happens at a much later date (five, ten, fifteen years or even further down the line).

There's no particular order to this chapter since we'll cover many topics, and then you'll decide which ones to investigate. Also, my knowledge being mainly based on the system in the UK and Italy, you should then really research the system in your own country.

What I want to show you here is a WAY OF THINKING rather than the specific numbers which might even be incorrect. However, if, after accepting that you'll have to do some paperwork, you start to enjoy the puzzle-logic of taxes and laws, national and international, you can really have some fun!

Many people rarely think about taxes and money and they just assume that they're not paying that much, that there's nothing they can do about it, that it's a boring matter, and that, after all, unless you're making a lot of money, it doesn't make a difference.

Income Tax – Basics

In most countries you pay taxes. These are mainly used to contribute to some public services and to help politicians and lawmakers in distress to make some good money with consultancy fees, commissions, public tenders and similar shenanigans. For this reason, it's very important to pay all the taxes that you have to pay and not a cent more.

Introduction

In the UK there are four bands of taxation:

UK Income Tax for the Financial Year 2020

Income (£)	Percentage of taxes you pay	Description
0 – 12,500	0%	Personal allowance
12,501 – 50,000	20%	Basic rate
50,001 – 150,000	40%	Higher rate
Above 150,000	45%	Additional rate

This means that, on the first £12,500 you earn in the UK, you don't pay any Income Tax; on the money that you earn between £12,501 – £50,000, you pay 20% Income Tax, and so on.

Example 1

Mary earns £12,500 every year, this means that:

- The yearly cost of National Insurance is £360
- She'll pay an Income Tax of £0
- She'll take home £12,140 every year (which is £1,011.67 per month)

Example 2

Mary earns £20,000 every year, this means that:

- She pays £0 Income Tax on the portion of her income between 0 and £12,500
- She'll pay 20% tax on the rest of her income (£7,500)
- Which means she'll pay £1,500 per year of Income Tax
- The yearly cost of National Insurance will be £1,260
- She'll take home £17,240, which is £1,436.67 per month

The Financial Year

In the UK, the financial year goes from the 6th of April to the 5th of April of the following year. This means that from a taxation point of view what is important is the money that you get between those two dates.

This piece of information might make you think: "So what?" but it has got some important implications.

The Financial Year and The Income Tax

Let's assume that Mary has started to work on the 1st of January 2020 at Such-and-Such company for a wage of £12,500, after a long period of inactivity and that her income doesn't change at all for some time after that.

From the 1st of January to the 5th of April, she'll pay 0% Income Tax, because she'll be well below the £12,500 threshold.

Then from the 6th of April 2020 to the 5th of April 2021, she'll still pay 0% Income Tax, because she's within the £12,500 threshold. During this year, Mary started to give Spanish language lessons and has earned a trading income of around £990 pounds in that financial year, which is less than the £1,000 threshold, so that falls in the tax free allowance.

Almost another year goes by, we're on the 30th of March now, and Mary:

- is still on £12,500 from her main employment but she's been made redundant
- she's earned around £950 from the Spanish language lessons
- she's about to start some group classes that will bring her a few thousand pounds
- and she's going to sell the year-long course to around one hundred people in one go who are ready to pay in advance within a few days' time

Mary is a smart girl and she talks with an accountant who then suggests waiting until after the 6th of April to make the big sale. Why?

- Mary is going to be out of work soon, the situation is grim, and she might struggle to find another job soon
- If she sells £10,000 worth of courses (£100 x 100 people) on the 30th of March, she'll pay 20% tax on that income (around £2,000). If she waits until the 6th of April, she'll pay 0%, unless in that financial year she finds another job and earns more money (above the £12,500 threshold).

Let this concept sink in for a moment.

By simply **timing** things properly, Mary just saved £2,000 which, at her current job, takes around two months of full-time work to earn. Now, if you're Mary, can you afford to pay that money in that situation? Can you really afford to pay £2,000 more taxes than you should? And, above all:

Can you afford not to know this stuff?

If you want to make money and you're saving on eating out, you're bulk-buying food, cutting on holidays, and working hard… well, you must know and understand money and taxation. That's as simple as that.

Married couples

Obviously, the more money you're moving, the more fun this becomes. Let's say that you're a couple and one of you has earned £10,000 for the year and the other has earned £13,500. This couple can use something called 'Marriage Allowance' which basically allows you to transfer up to £1,000 from one salary to the other to bring it below a threshold and pay less taxes.

In simple terms: £13,500 - £1,000 = £12,500, so now this person is below the threshold; and the other person in the couple gets £10,000 + £1,000 = £11,000, which is also still below the threshold. All of a sudden you save around £200 which is probably equivalent to almost one week of work at that income level.

Renting a room (or more) in your house

Let's go back to Xiaohui and Jenny. We know that as soon as they bought their house, they rented out a room. They were able, thanks to the local laws, to rent the room and earn £3,600 tax-free.

In the UK, you can rent out a room in your main house and earn up to £7,500 tax-free (in 2020). In other countries this might not apply but is still an interesting option for young people and, depending on who owns the house, you might still pay little or no taxes.

If you have a house with three bedrooms, you might decide to rent two out and get the full £7,500 tax-free.

Incomes, properties and taxes

A short sad story

People want to own things and the same goes for couples. So, when Xiaohui and Jenny decided to start their wealth journey, they decided to buy their first house by sharing the ownership 50/50 and also getting a mortgage at 50/50. It seemed the reasonable choice at the time and, given the fact that things can change between people, it probably was.

A few years go by and now they have five properties, all of them split 50/50. They live in one of them and they get rental income from the other four. In order to 'play safe' they've gone for long fixed-term mortgages (ten years) on each one of the rental properties so they're in a fixed deal for ten, eight, seven and six years. Moreover, they're still on a seven year fixed deal on their main property. Jenny is pregnant and they've decided that, after the birth of their first child, she won't go back to work and will take care of the baby and help Xiaohui more with their business. Xiaohui's business is doing well and he's also getting good money working as a consultant from his previous employer.

Suddenly they realise they have a problem.

Xiaohui is earning almost £50,000 per year from his consultancy work thanks to some big projects that required his specific skills. At the same time, the rental properties are doing well and bringing a TAXABLE INCOME (after you've deducted all the allowable expenses) of £1,300 per month and £15,600 per year. Now, this income is split between Jenny and Xiaohui since they're both owners of the properties, which means that £7,800 of this income is attributable to Jenny and £7,800 to Xiaohui.

Now, Jenny has stopped working and, for that financial year, she's below the £12,500 threshold so she pays no taxes at all on the £7,800. On the other hand, Xiaohui is already at £50,000, so he ends up paying the 40% tax rate on the additional £7,800 and this means that he pays £3,120 in taxes. Repeat this for ten years and Xiaohui would be paying in excess of £30,000 of taxes on the rental income alone (actually more and more as the mortgages on the properties decrease and the profit increases).

He starts to look for solutions and he realises that the situation is more complicated than he thought: he wanted to gift the properties to his wife so that all the rental income went to her, but these properties have mortgages attached, fixed terms and early repayment charges, which make the gifting a very expensive operation.

Xiaohui and Jenny realise, perhaps too late, that they should have planned this more carefully, keeping in mind their tax position, but who's really thinking about taxes when you're starting up your own company, working full-time, trying to live, and buying and renting properties? Very few people, unless they have the guidance that I'm offering you in this book.

We'll look at some of the possible solutions, however, let's first look at which taxes are associated with owning and renting out properties.

Income streams and taxes

If you have four different sources of income (employed, self-employed, rental and investments), generally speaking, all the money that you earn goes towards your income, which is then taxed accordingly. For example, if we look at Xiaohui, we see that he earns:
- £50,000 from consultancy with his previous employer (basically he is self-employed)
- £7,800 from rental income
- £15,000 from his own business
- £2,200 from investment

You might think that he's earning a lot of money but, on the £25,000 he makes above £50,000, he's paying 40% tax (£10,000).

Rental income

Rental income is part of your general income so, in most countries, you pay income tax on it. Obviously, if there are some expenses associated with running your small property empire, these can be deducted and, for this reason, it's important to understand what these expenses are and keep track of them. As always, your accountant is the best person to ask in these cases.

Also, if you own the property 50/50 with your partner, as far as the income tax is concerned, the rental income is split among the two of you. This means that, in some cases when one person is nearer to the tax threshold than the other, it might not make sense to split the property in half but it might be better for only one person to be the sole owner.

For example, if Xiaohui earns close to £50,000 and Jenny earns £0, it would make sense for the properties to be in Jenny's name so that the rental income is not taxed at a higher level.

This also means, however, that if Jenny falls in love with Mark and leaves Xiaohui, Xiaohui might well lose the whole property portfolio. As with everything, there are pros and cons.

Finally, in some cases, losses in one year can be offset against profit of the next year, however, we all hope that this will never be the case.

Stamp Duty – Pay when you buy

In the UK, as in many other jurisdictions, the simple fact of buying a house accrues some taxes. In the UK, this tax is known as Stamp Duty Land Tax (SDLT) and it looks like:

Property Value	SDLT - First Home	SDLT – Additional property
< £125,000	0%	3%
£125,000 - £250,000	2%	5%
£250,000 - £925,000	5%	8%
£925,000 - £1,500,000	10%	13%
> £1,500,000	12%	15%

This table means that on your first home, if it costs below £125,000, you pay 0% of SDLT. If you buy a £200,000 first home, you pay 0% on the portion below £125,000 and 2% on the portion between £125,000 and £200,000 (£1,500). This is a one-off payment and you pay this when you buy the house, not when you sell it.

This also mean that, as you start to buy your second, third and fourth houses, you'll pay a higher rate. For example, on a £120,000 second home, you'll pay 3% (£3,000+).

Now, if we go back to Xiaohui and Jenny, they bought their first home at 50/50 which means that they both own the house so, when they buy the second home, it's the second home for both of them so they will pay SDLT at the additional rate. On the other hand, if Jenny had bought the first house alone and then Xiaohui also had bought alone, then SDLT would not apply to either, potentially saving them thousands.

You could write a book about this, the concept again is: would you like to earn £3,000+ when you buy a £125,000 home? If the answer is YES, study your country's taxes.

Capital Gains Tax (CGT) – Pay when you sell

Let's imagine you bought the house alone for £100,000, and ten years later you sell it for £135,000. You might naively think that you earn £35,000 or something along those lines, perhaps assuming that you'll pay some commission to an agent that you might not need, along with some other expenses.

Unfortunately for you, in most countries, if you, as an individual, make a gain because the value of your capital increases, you pay taxes on in. In the UK in 2020, if you're a basic rate taxpayer you pay 18% tax. If you're a higher rate taxpayer (> £50,000) you'll end up **paying a whopping 28%**.

As with everything, the devil is in the detail. Each year you have a so-called Capital Gains Tax-Free allowance which means that you can make £12,300 worth of capital gains tax-free. So, if you bought the house for £100,000 and you sell it for £112,300, you won't pay any CGT.

Also, if the property is your main residence you don't pay CGT when you sell it, but then if you have four properties and you want to sell them all, you should actually live in each one for at least a year or two before selling them in order to benefit from this scheme and, still, it might be seen as tax avoidance so, as always, consult a professional.

If you've spent money on renovations (a new bathroom, an extension etc.), these expenses could be detracted from the amount that then would be subject to CGT. The same goes for solicitor and estate agent fees, the stamp duty that you paid when you bought the house, and so forth.

Inheritance Tax (IHT) – Pay when you die

In the UK, there's a well-known tax called the Inheritance Tax, which is a tax that your children pay when you leave them an inheritance of more than £325,000 (UK, 2020). On the portion above that number they'll pay 40% tax.

For example, if you only have one big home, mortgage-free, worth £1,325,000, and, at the end of your life, you leave it to your children with nothing else, they'll have to pay £330,000 of inheritance tax. Obviously, there are legal ways to optimise this. Again, can you afford not to know this early on when you start to structure your wealth?

Lawmakers' imagination

In these pages I'm simply trying to scare the life out of you.

You were twenty years old and trying to save £20 by not eating out; thirty-five years go by and you're fifty-five and, all of a sudden, a string of characters on a piece of paper called 'The Law' mean that you have to pay tens or even hundreds of thousands of pounds every time you do anything with your money: you buy an investment and you pay money, you sell it and you pay, you die and your kids pay, you rent out and you pay, you make money from interests and you pay: it soon becomes a tax inferno.

The UK is a very good place when it comes to taxes and a relatively fair system, but you can still end up paying a lot of taxes. Imagine what happens in countries with a heavy taxation.

For example, in Italy, a country with very creative and artistic lawmakers, you pay a tax, every year, for the simple fact of owning a property. So, if you have three houses, even if you don't get any rental income, you'll still be subject to this tax called IMU which, in the worst case scenario, is around 0.76% of the value of the house (760 euros every year if you have a house worth 100,000 euros). Ode to Joy! In some places like Thailand, you can't own a house if you're a foreigner which means that what we discussed would be very complicated to do. In some other countries, there are limitations on the rent you can charge, or you get charged if the property sits empty and so on.

Now, don't get me wrong, as I said before: we all want to help politicians and lawmakers in distress, so we'll always pay all the taxes that we have to pay and nothing more. The money that you save in taxes can be reinvested in your business and used to create workplaces for young and aspiring people.

The light at the end of the tunnel: for you, for the lawmakers and for Xiaohui

Luckily, real communism doesn't really exist.

As in the novel *Animal Farm* by George Orwell where the animals, following the lead of the pigs, revolt against the human oppression only to find out years later that the pigs turn into the humans; in almost all countries and systems, the political class that "wants" to stop loopholes for legal tax avoidance, creates those very loopholes in the legislative structure that allows them (and you) to legally pay less taxes.

Many people in politics have some financial interests to protect and, while some of them will genuinely try to make everybody pay their fair share of taxes, the majority in many places still try to keep openings for themselves to avoid paying the full bill.

This is one of the reasons why some billion-pound companies pay little taxes, why people with net-worths of billions of pounds pay no inheritance tax, and so on. So, let's follow the examples set by the leaders, learn from them and follow the same clever strategies that they've put in place for themselves.

A solution for Xiaohui

So, if you re-read what happened to Xiaohui, you might think that there's no way out. If we look at his income and Jenny's income and how they structured their property ownership, it could seem that he either accepts paying more taxes to make more money, or he can work less, earn less, have more free time and pay less taxes. Luckily, there's another option: he has his own business.

After talking with his accountant, the accountant suggests that his previous company could buy the consultancy services he's offering from his limited company rather than paying him on a self-employed basis. In this way, the £50,000 (or part of it) will be part of the profit of his company rather than his personal taxable income, until taken out. This gives Xiaohui a way forward and helps him to save tens of thousands of pounds in taxes that he then can invest to grow his own business and his own limited company.
This concept is important:

You and a limited company are separate entities

and this means that, as long as your accountant agrees, you can use the limited company as a way to optimise how your money is taxed, managed, invested and grown. Obviously, if the devil is in the detail when it comes to personal finances, things get even more complicated when you talk about company finance and company law.

The Company

As I've emphasised many times over the course of these pages, while you study, specialise, save money, and buy the first and second property to build some basic wealth, it's with your own company that you can build some serious wealth.

As an individual, you:

- Get paid a salary
- Pay taxes on it (Income Tax, National Insurance)
- And then, with the money that you have left, you then pay for things and investments

As a company, there's a big difference which is:

- The company gets some money from doing business
- The company then buys everything else that it needs (including other's people work in the form of a wage)
- And then, and only then, if there's any money left in real profit, it pays taxes on it

This means that by setting up a limited company, you're not only separating the risks of the company from your own personal risks, but you now have an extremely useful tool to grow wealth.

This means that, in theory, as long as the money stays in the company and you keep re-investing it, you can pay very little tax, so the wealth generation can be accelerated.

It's for this very same reason that I strongly recommended keeping your main job for as long as possible: the longer you don't need to pay yourself a salary (plunder your own company), the more you can reinvest and grow your company, the quicker it can grow.

Companies also have some other wonderful perks. For example, you pay Corporation Tax, which is the tax on the profit which is left in the company after all the costs and salaries have been paid. At the moment in England, Corporation Tax is

19% (which is 1% lower than the Income Tax for a basic rate earner and 21% lower for a higher rate earner).

However, companies don't pay Capital Gains Tax on the sale of a property, so this means that if you plan to grow your property portfolio by buying and selling, then it makes a lot of sense to do it through a company if, let's say, you have four or more properties.

Once your company (or companies) have some solid footing, you can then start to pay yourself a salary. As you remember, below £12,500 you pay 0% Income Tax which means that both Xiaohui and Jenny could get £12,500 each per year almost tax-free (£2,000+ per month).

Moreover, they're both directors and shareholders in the company which means that they can take money out as a dividend and pay no taxes on the first £2,000 for the year (each) and then, if they're at the basic rate (<£50,000), they then pay 7.5% tax on dividends rather than 20%... and so on and on and on.

International dreams and taxes

Xiaohui and Jenny have always dreamt about moving abroad, and now, thanks to their property portfolio, their own business, some work they do as consultants, and some other investments, they decide to move to France. A few days before their move a friend asks them: "What about the taxes?"

In fact, when you move to another country and you stay more than six months and one day in the other country, you usually automatically become a fiscal resident (from a taxation point of view) in that other country and you will be taxed on your worldwide income.

This has certainly got some interesting implications: you might have created something that works perfectly in the US, but then it doesn't work when you move to Germany, because of the fiscal environment.

Moreover, moving from one country to the other and having properties, businesses and incomes from different sources complicates matters even more. In some countries you'll be taxed when you get dividends from your company based abroad, in some other countries you'll be taxed on worldwide properties, in some others again you'll be taxed twice and so on.

International taxation and living abroad or even in two countries can be a dream, however, it requires a lot of planning and preparation and you need to make sure that you're based where you will be treated best.
Message

The message of this chapter is simple: do not let all your hard-earned money go to waste because you can't be bothered to plan accordingly. We saw that Mary could save £2,000 and that Xiaohui could save tens of thousands of pounds. How long does it take you to save that money? A year? Six months? Two years?

Now sit down, relax, and enjoy spending two months learning about taxes – you will have earned months and years of life.

Level 5

*Today is the first day of the rest of your life.
Go and make a lot of money*

Conclusion

Dear Reader,

You are now an investor and a businessman.

We're now at the end of this book so I can tell you that Level 5 was never intended to be written.

How could I tell you how to become the next revolutionary who is going to create a value-generating empire if I haven't done it myself? Can the level of wealth attained by Bill Gates, Jeff Bezos, Elon Musk and similar characters really be predicted? Engineered? Standardised in a sequence of steps?

Are there objective limitations to the chances of each one of us to attain that level of wealth and influence?

It's very difficult to give an answer to these questions.

If you follow and expand on the advice in this book, it will bring you to the point where you'll be wealthy and free, possibly in less than ten years.

It will then be up to you how you use this wealth and freedom to improve this world that, more than money and wealth, needs us all to stop and smell the roses.

Good luck and now…

        go and make some money, you know how now.

Mr. Bill Silverstone…just a pen name!

        Completed at 00:00 on the

        20/08/2020

www.ingramcontent.com/pod-product-compliance
Lightning Source LLC
Chambersburg PA
CBHW081425220526
45466CB00008B/2276